THE VOLUNTARY WORKER IN THE SOCIAL SERVICES

National Institute for Social Work Training series no. 16
National Council of Social Service publication 787

National Institute for Social Work Training
MARY WARD HOUSE, TAVISTOCK PLACE, LONDON, W.C.1.
National Council of Social Service (Incorporated)
26 BEDFORD SQUARE, LONDON, W.C.1.

THE VOLUNTARY WORKER
IN THE
SOCIAL SERVICES

Report of a Committee jointly set up by the
National Council of Social Service and
the National Institute for Social Work Training
under the Chairmanship of
GERALDINE M. AVES
C.B.E.

London
THE BEDFORD SQUARE PRESS OF THE NCSS
AND
GEORGE ALLEN AND UNWIN LTD

PRINTED IN GREAT BRITAIN
in 11 on 12pt Times type
BY ALDEN AND MOWBRAY LTD
AT THE ALDEN PRESS, OXFORD

MEMBERS OF THE COMMITTEE
OF ENQUIRY

MISS GERALDINE M. AVES, C.B.E.	Chairman
HUGH BARR	Director, Teamwork Associates: a pilot project in prison after-care. (Co-opted February 1968)
MISS JOAN EASTMAN	Lecturer in Social Work, University of Exeter
ALAN GIBSON	Head, The Youth Service Information Centre (to March 1969). (Co-opted February 1968)
MISS E. M. GOLDBERG	Director of Research, National Institute for Social Work Training
ROY A. JACKSON	Director of Studies, Trades Union Congress
MISS ELISABETH LITTLEJOHN, J.P.	Secretary, Standing Conference of Councils of Social Service. National Council of Social Service
H. MORRIS-JONES	Professor and Head of the Department of Social Theory and Institutions, University College of North Wales, Bangor
R. S. J. POTTER	County Welfare Officer, Hertfordshire County Council
E. G. PRATT	Assistant Principal Probation Officer, Inner London Probation and After-care Service
MRS W. E. RIDDELL	Voluntary Worker. Chairman, Ealing Association for Mental Health
MISS HELEN ROBERTS, O.B.E.	Secretary, Sheffield Diocesan Social Responsibility Council
JEF SMITH	Deputy Secretary-General, International Voluntary Service. Since January 1969, Senior Child Care Officer, London Borough of Haringey
MISS G. M. WANS-BROUGH-JONES, O.B.E.	Hon. Secretary from May 1968

MEMBERS OF THE WORKING PARTY ON PREPARATION AND TRAINING

MISS GERALDINE M. AVES, C.B.E.	Chairman
HUGH BARR	Teamwork Associates
ALAN GIBSON	The Youth Service Information Centre
ROY A. JACKSON	Member of main Committee
MISS ALICE JOHNSTON, C.B.E.	Women's Royal Voluntary Service
MISS JACQUELINE M. KNIGHT	British Red Cross Society
MISS ELISABETH LITTLEJOHN, J.P.	Member of main Committee
MRS EDITH MORGAN	National Association for Mental Health
MRS DENISE NEWMAN	National Old People's Welfare Council
MRS EVE ROAD	Blackfriars Family Counsellors Project
JEF SMITH	Member of main Committee

Acknowledgements

As a Committee we wish to place on record our appreciation of the unfailing support and confidence we have received from our sponsors.

We wish also to express our thanks for the energetic and unstinted help given by Mrs Elizabeth Pearce, our secretary until April 1968, Mrs Rose Deakin, assistant secretary and investigator, and Mrs Audrey Lemmon. Mr George Churcher, Registrar of the National Institute for Social Work Training, has kindly acted as Bursar and has relieved us of all anxiety with regard to account-keeping and the general state of our finances.

We wish to refer particularly to the contribution of Miss G. M. Wansbrough-Jones, who has analysed a mass of material and presented it in a logical and lucid way. She has devoted the greater part of her first year of retirement, in which she had planned to enjoy some leisure, to the gruelling task of helping us to formulate this Report. We find it difficult to convey our gratitude in adequate terms.

G. M. AVES
Chairman

Foreword

There is a great tradition of voluntary service in the United Kingdom and, in spite of all the rapid changes in our society, the impulse to serve is still strong and widespread. Yet, while much has been written about the role of the voluntary organizations in the future, there has been relatively little study of the role of the individual voluntary worker. Clearly there is a need to recruit, train and deploy volunteers willing to give personal service; but how can they fit into the total structure of the social services and what should be their relationship to professional workers?

These questions led the National Council of Social Service jointly with the National Institute for Social Work Training to set up an independent committee of enquiry in 1966 to study the role of voluntary workers in the social services. The joint venture was made possible by generous financial support from the Joseph Rowntree Memorial Trust and the Phyllis Trust, to which our grateful thanks are due.

The Council and the Institute were fortunate in securing the aid of a Committee, under the chairmanship of Miss G. M. Aves, formerly Chief Welfare Officer of the Ministry of Health. The members, all of whom served in a personal capacity, brought to the task a wide range of knowledge and experience in the social welfare field. We are grateful to them for the immense amount of patience and care with which they have tackled their task. Specifically, we would like to thank Miss Aves for guiding the venture so skilfully to a successful fruition, as well as all those who made this possible, including those who gave evidence or answered questionnaires and otherwise helped with the enquiry.

While we cannot commit our respective Councils before they have studied the Report, we appreciate the great importance of its contents and its recommendations. We hope that the Report will be widely distributed and that the Government, the local authorities, the professional social workers, the voluntary organizations and all those interested in the social services, not least the volunteers themselves, will give it the serious study which it so obviously deserves.   L. FARRER-BROWN

Chairman, National Council of Social Service

FREDERIC SEEBOHM

Chairman, National Institute for Social Work Training

Contents

Chapter 1

INTRODUCTION

1   This Committee was set up in June 1966 by the National Council of Social Service and the National Institute for Social Work Training with the following terms of reference: 'to enquire into the role of voluntary workers in the social services and in particular to consider their need for preparation or training and their relationship with professional social workers'. The scope of the enquiry was to be confined to England and Wales. The sponsors were not seeking to inspire an elaborate research project, but they recognized the urgent need to examine the contribution made by volunteers to the work of voluntary and statutory bodies. Was this contribution welcomed? Was it expanding or diminishing in size or in quality? Was it intelligently used? Was the traditional pioneer obsolescent? Was the field of recruitment changing? These and a host of other questions needed examination.

2   Since the terms of reference place special emphasis on the training of volunteers and their relationship with professionally qualified social workers, the Committee decided to restrict its study, in the main, to what may be termed the field work setting. We excluded from our consideration the role of volunteers as money raisers, or as committee members or administrators, important and interesting as these are as subjects for study. Reluctantly we left them for the attention of some other body. Magistrates are another important group, whom for similar reasons we have deliberately omitted. Consideration of the role of the volunteer as an element in the aggregation of services that seek to meet personal needs, with all that this implies in terms of recruitment, training, deployment, relationships and the development of new services, already offered an

15

extensive field for enquiry. Nor did it seem practicable to make any serious examination of the experience of other countries, though some material from the United States was studied and two United Nations seminars in 1966 and 1967 provided welcome illustrations of the stage which European countries have reached.

3   Another omission is that of foster parents. This is not due to any lack of appreciation of their work, or of the strong voluntary element which it contains. This work is, however, specialized, and very different in many respects from that of the volunteers whom we are considering. As attention has been given elsewhere to foster parents and their work, we decided that it would not be appropriate to include them in our study.

4   We saw the need for our enquiry as anything but an academic one. Social services had become more comprehensive and more complex than ever before, and there was increasing realization of the part that they needed to play. The aims of the services were becoming more explicit; their limitations as well as their potentialities were more clearly realized; shortages of suitably equipped staff were constantly deplored, and there were doubts about the wisdom—even if it had been practicable—of trying to meet all these needs by the use of paid staff. In short, it had become apparent that only by the intelligent mobilization of every resource could society hope to realize its aspirations to meet a very wide range of human needs. Among these resources the services available from volunteers clearly needed careful evaluation.

5   The membership of the Committee reflects a wide range of interests, both academic and professional, but although many of the members have undertaken voluntary work at some time, most of them are no longer directly engaged in it. We therefore took early steps to inform ourselves as well as possible about the current situation. We set ourselves to discover something about the practice of voluntary work, and attitudes towards it from different angles, from bodies that used volunteers to a greater or less degree, and from organizations both of professional workers

and of those concerned with the administration of the social services. Questionnaires were sent to these bodies, and the knowledge so obtained was reinforced by meetings held by two or more members of the Committee with a variety of groups of social workers or volunteers, who discussed informally, and with agreeable frankness, their experience in different settings. The reactions of the recipients of the services seemed to us of special importance and a modest investigation illuminated this aspect of the subject. This knowledge was further enriched by studies undertaken, either on behalf of the Committee, or in consultation with it; and lastly we were given ready access to other current and as yet unpublished investigations. A list of these various sources is given in Appendix III.

6   We found it necessary to differentiate between those who are qualified to undertake social work professionally, and volunteers who are without this qualification. Now that the majority of those belonging to the profession of social work have formed a single association, the British Association of Social Workers, it is increasingly accepted that they are the people to whom the term 'social worker' properly applies. We have there- fore used the term in this sense throughout this report. We also discussed the use of various terms for those who receive the help of the social services and of volunteers—'recipients', 'consumers', 'clients', and others; and decided that 'clients', though not ideal, was preferable to any of the alternatives.

7   The importance of the preparation or training of volun- teers, to which special attention was to be directed, seemed to justify enlisting the collaboration of persons who were closely informed about current practices and at the same time pre- pared to take a new and critical look at them. A working party was accordingly set up consisting of five co-opted members and three members of the main Committee. Their study of the training issues was most valuable as a contribution to this report.

8   We would like to express now with great sincerity our appreciation of the help which we have received at all stages from

the bodies and individuals whose co-operation we sought. The answering of questionnaires is tiresome and time-consuming, yet two-thirds of the voluntary organizations to which we sent a long questionnaire responded. The nature of these organizations was such that, while some were able to send a single reply, others had to obtain information from a number of local branches or affiliated bodies (see Appendix II). In all, 267 completed questionnaires were returned to us. If they were not all as illuminating as had been hoped, this is partly because we may have had unduly high expectations of what could be gained from a somewhat elaborate questionnaire. Moreover, in an effort to temper the wind to the shorn lamb, an escape clause gave organizations a chance to limit the extent of their response. When it was a question of meeting and talking with individuals or groups of invariably over-busy workers (since that is a characteristic of the social services today) their readiness to share in the Committee's explorations was always generous and immediate.

9 The Committee has had difficulty in not feeling overwhelmed by the breadth of the potential subject and the modesty of its resources. We have undertaken our enquiries at a time when a succession of reports, massive in their importance, and often in their documentation, have been before the country, some of which have demonstrated the value of sophisticated techniques of research and investigation. Moreover, most of the Committees responsible for these reports have had at their disposal the administrative and clerical resources of central departments. These resources were not available to us, and it therefore became imperative to limit the sphere of our enquiry to something that could reasonably be encompassed. Today there are few personal social services where some contribution by voluntary workers is not apparent. A study that examined in detail their relevance in all the services involved would have resulted in a voluminous report of discouraging price and complexity, and we have, therefore, been obliged to concentrate mainly on principles and methods which are of general application. For the most part our attention has been devoted to the part played by volunteers in various settings, the influences which lead to their offers of service, and the efforts currently made to

18

maintain and develop their interest; and we have tried to suggest ways in which society might gain more widely from the rich reserve of kindliness and goodwill that characterizes our people.

10   We are extremely conscious of the fine line that divides some of the work done by volunteers from that carried out by numberless friends and neighbours, who become aware of individual needs and meet them in a completely informal and unorganized way. These tasks are often shouldered, to an extent that is insufficiently recognized, by relatives if there are any, and by the friendly neighbour where there is a gap to be filled. We believe this spontaneous response to need to be one of the strengths of our society, and we wish to make it abundantly clear at the outset that nothing we have to say about voluntary workers, their recruitment or their training, is intended to detract from the spontaneous contribution of the neighbour; indeed, quite the contrary. But this brief reference to the importance of the good neighbour may perhaps explain why it seemed desirable to focus our attention mainly on the role of the volunteer within the framework of some form of organization, and this we have sought to do.

11   We decided, as a matter of convenience, to use the terms 'volunteer' and 'voluntary worker' in this report as synonymous, though we fully realize that in other contexts they may carry somewhat different meanings. People are sometimes referred to, and regard themselves, as volunteers who are certainly not voluntary workers; for example those who, having offered to assist in a service, receive payment which is comparable with that earned by regular employees in a similar field; and these we naturally exclude. We do not, however, see any difficulty in including among voluntary workers those young volunteers, many of whom have no paid employment, who receive a token payment in respect of the service which they give as members of voluntary organizations. In general we found that it was not possible to formulate any neat definition of a voluntary worker, and came to the conclusion that there was no merit in attempting to restrict the term in any precise way. Just as we have seen

no clear dividing line between the good neighbour and the volunteer, so we found indeterminate areas in other directions, in community work and in the work contributed voluntarily by professional people from many fields—law, medicine, social work and education, to quote only a few. It is, after all, not the object of our enquiry to scrutinize and classify volunteers in a way that appears to limit their spheres of activity. Indeed, the reverse is the case. Later, we attempt to define their role in a consistent way, because only so can we formalize our findings and our recommendations. At this point we want to record our determination to preserve a very open attitude to what may properly be regarded as voluntary work. We have also resisted the temptation to estimate the total number engaged in voluntary work in England and Wales today; though in Chapter 3 (paragraph 43) we quote some figures which relate to certain aspects of the work, and which may give some indication of its scale.

12   It is no doubt a matter of embarrassment to all committees of enquiry that life does not stand still while they pursue their investigations. During this Committee's period of study, new pioneer organizations making extensive use of voluntary help have made their appearance, and the attention devoted by older organizations and by professional workers to the role of volunteers has undoubtedly increased. We would certainly not wish to suggest that this is an example of cause and effect, though we can reasonably claim that the very process of asking questions has its repercussions. We have seen and greatly welcomed constant evidence of lively interest in the subject of our enquiry.

13   We are under no illusions about the wealth of study yet to be undertaken, both on some of the subject matter central to this enquiry and on other matters highly germane to it. We quickly became aware, in particular, of the need for further study of the role of voluntary organizations in the field of the social services. We were interested to note the many references in the Report of the Committee on Local Authority and Allied Personal Social Services (the Seebohm Report) to the impor-

tance of involving the community, and mobilizing all the community's resources to provide help for those members who need it. This, although not the central theme of that Report, constantly recurs, and is typified by the following statement early in the Report (para. 139):

'The ways in which existing resources are organized and deployed are inefficient. Much more ought to be done in the fields of prevention, community involvement, the guidance of voluntary workers, and in making fuller use of voluntary organizations.'

14   There are signs that some readers have interpreted parts of the Seebohm Report as decrying the contribution of voluntary organizations; particularly, perhaps, the suggestion that local authorities need to make more direct use of voluntary workers, but that 'meanwhile there are advantages in working through existing voluntary organizations which would recruit the volunteers'. We are satisfied that this was not the intention of the Seebohm Committee; and we think it important, therefore, to state categorically that we believe any development in the direct use of volunteers by statutory bodies is likely to result in an increased recognition of the contribution of voluntary effort, including that of voluntary organizations, provided that they, too, can move with the times. We have seen that a number of them are already demonstrating their ability to do this, and, having paid special attention to growth points in the use of voluntary help, we have based many of our proposals on our examination of some of the more recent developments. We try to indicate, in ways that are appropriate to our particular terms of reference, how further progress might be made.

Chapter 2

THE BACKGROUND TO
VOLUNTARY WORK TODAY

15   We do not propose to preface our report with a history of voluntary work. We believe our readers will accept, as the Seebohm Committee did, that in our developing personal social services, the volunteer has a significant role. This role may need to be re-examined and re-defined, but it exists as it has done throughout our history. In the setting of the Welfare State, which makes more public provision for need than has ever before been experienced in this country, the great increase of interest in the contribution of volunteers to the social services may at first seem paradoxical. It is, however, as we have already suggested, because society's expectations of these services are so high that the support of volunteers is seen to be essential if expectations are to be realized. Moreover, it appears that the process of becoming an advanced industrial society has had effects which contribute to the interest in voluntary work. The degree of control over parts of our lives and the loss of some of the personal element, particularly at work, have produced a desire to counteract these effects by undertaking activities which give scope for spontaneity, initiative and contact with other people.

16   After the struggles at the turn of the century between the adherents of either voluntary or statutory provision as the principal agent of social support, we have seen the gradual development of a partnership. Although we are left with some services where the independent role of the voluntary organization remains unimpaired, the main feature of the current scene is the ever increasing responsibility of statutory bodies for meeting individual needs, and their growing awareness of their own need for voluntary reinforcements. A partnership of some

kind inevitably develops. It usually grows out of some experience of working together; and the relationship varies considerably, both in its nature and in its structure, according to the service, the area of work undertaken under voluntary auspices, and the responsibilities and attitudes of the central or local authority concerned.

17   Some of the pioneers of social services, such as Octavia Hill, in housing management, and C. S. Loch of the Charity Organization Society were also alive to the importance of training, but, although many types of social work have their origins in the nineteenth century, it is only in the last fifty years that they have been placed on a professional footing. Now the qualified social worker has emerged as an influence to be reckoned with in the further development of the social services. The numbers of trained workers have conspicuously increased, and their spheres of activity constantly widen. Narrowly specialized functions are giving way to a broad interpretation of their professional role, and a restricted view of their responsibilities as agents of social change to the acceptance of social action as a legitimate concern.

18   Because the range of the social services and the scope of social work have increased much more rapidly than the supply of trained workers, volunteers are readily seen to be important as a support to overburdened services. They have also continued, as members of voluntary organizations, to perform the function of filling some of the gaps in the statutory services. They have, however, another and even more important role. They are one means by which the community itself can participate in discovering and meeting the needs of its members; and the wider the field of recruitment for volunteers, the more significant this is. Also, since voluntary workers do not need to concern themselves with administrative distinctions they can ignore the boundaries between services, and concentrate on human needs.

19   Over the years volunteers have continued to extend their contribution, and answers to our questionnaire to social agencies show an astonishing spread of service offered. However, apart

from a few notable exceptions, such as the Ministry of Social Security War Pensions scheme, the Youth Service and the London School Care Committee service, volunteers tended until the nineteen-sixties to work as members of voluntary organizations, even when they were working within a statutory setting, such as a hospital. The origin of the Women's Royal Voluntary Service illustrates the extent to which this was an acceptable pattern since, although financed from the Exchequer and founded primarily to assist local authorities in the field of Civil Defence, it has retained a separate organization and identity.

20   At different stages in different services there have been fluctuations in the attitudes of committees of management and of social workers to the contribution of volunteers. The recent history of the Family Welfare Association and of the Invalid Children's Aid Association illustrates this point. We have seen a swing from maximum use of volunteers to maximum use of trained staff; and now, possibly, the beginning of a trend back again to greater recognition of the volunteer's role. In the statutory services, where the majority of social workers are now employed, their attitude to volunteers has become of crucial importance.

21   Side by side with the growth of partnership between public and private agencies, we see by way of contrast a remarkable series of independent pioneering efforts, which reproduce, sometimes with equally dramatic effect, the pioneer movements of the past. Victorian efforts, like those on behalf of prisoners, prostitutes, orphaned or unwanted children, have their counterpart today in a steady flow of attempts to reach those who somehow remain largely untouched by the complex network of statutory services, meths. drinkers, itinerants, rudderless young people, and so forth. The new and heartening characteristic of today's pioneers is that, unlike most of their predecessors, they start as a rule without social or financial privilege or an assumption that they are entitled to make moral judgments about their neighbours. The pioneering drive tends to come from the young, from egalitarians, from those who resent social dysfunctioning

and individual misery and have sufficiently passionate convictions to try to do something about it. There is evidence that such movements are able to draw upon a considerable supply of volunteers.

Young Volunteers

22   There are references throughout this report to services by young people and how they fit into the whole scheme of voluntary effort. Here we wish only to make a few general comments on the importance of their increasing interest in and contribution to voluntary work. We cannot define precisely the springs of voluntary action among young people, but it seems indisputable that there is at the moment a surge of idealism and of dissatisfaction with traditional social institutions which finds some outlet in increased voluntary work in the social services. Many young people are coming to realize the implicit link between the voluntary work they undertake and their concern over wider political issues. Some are inclined to turn away from what they identify as voluntary work, fearing it to be a patching-up of a situation requiring a more radical solution; but others recognize that it introduces them to fields in which action on other than political levels is also appropriate. There is clearly a link between this kind of motivation and that of members of pressure groups and social reformers.

23   Many of the questionnaires analysed for the Committee from organizations promoting service by youth showed evidence of imaginative attempts to widen the range of work and start experimental projects. We have already referred to the way in which much of the enthusiasm of young volunteers is directed towards independently seeking out and helping some of the most difficult groups in society. Schemes designed to promote community participation, which are in some areas sponsored by local authorities jointly with or through the agency of voluntary bodies, are often put into practice by young people's voluntary service schemes. The range of services undertaken is as wide as that of adult volunteers and, if anything, young people score for their flexibility in being willing to undertake any task. On the

one hand, they do not spurn purely practical or domestic jobs; on the other, they have sometimes surprised experienced social workers with the sophistication of their contribution in extremely complex situations. In their work with old people the ability of young volunteers to bridge the generation gap seems particularly valuable.

24   Having made these points, we do not propose to isolate young volunteers for separate treatment in the rest of this report. Young volunteers are essentially part of the whole picture and, in many respects, we find them to be distinguishable from their elders only by age. There is a good deal of resistance, not least from young people themselves, to regarding them as a separate group. Indeed, International Voluntary Service, one organization whose active members are for the most part young, stresses that its membership is equally open to older people, and that it particularly aims to break down barriers between age groups. Undesirable differentiation based on age can be seen in varying contexts. For instance, it is sometimes argued that it is good for young people to tackle a job on their own and, there-fore, the kind of preparation, introduction to a client, and back-ground knowledge that would be thought necessary for an older worker may be withheld from them. For young volunteers, as for all others, the overriding objective must be the good of the client. This does not mean that the flexible, informal and en-thusiastic approach of many young people should be restrained: indeed, this is greatly to be valued. Their short-term commitment may neither justify nor permit long-term methods of training; but appropriate preparation and guidance, as carefully thought out as for any other volunteer, should be available to them.

Self Help Movements

25   Some of the most effective developments in voluntary effort are to be found in organizations commonly described as of the 'self help' type. We regard self help as such as falling outside our terms of reference. Admittedly, it is difficult to say at what point self help becomes voluntary work in our sense; it is clear only that the precise boundary is hard to distinguish. We should,

however, consider it a serious omission if we failed to refer to the signal achievements of self help movements and the way in which they too have exercised a pioneering role. Alcoholics Anonymous, the National Society for Mentally Handicapped Children, and the Spastics Society, immediately spring to mind as classic examples; and new groups are constantly being formed, as for instance, Gamblers Anonymous, and the organization known as 'Release', which was started to help young people who were facing drug charges.

26   We observe that in their early stages self help groups tend to remain self-absorbed and somewhat isolated from the main stream of the social services. Their efforts to cater for a specialized type of need, and to demonstrate how this can be met, seem to make a degree of separatism almost inevitable for a time; and this is exemplified by limited use of volunteers from outside their own ranks and a tenuous relationship with other existing services. Some of the disadvantages of undue specialization, are that it runs counter to recognition of the common element in people's needs, and to increasing participation by the community in seeking to meet them. Some self help groups seem to remain apart, but others, as time goes on, become less isolated and more ready to form links with other services. This process may in some cases be assisted by a greater general understanding of the particular disability with which an organization is concerned, and a consequent lessening of the social stigma attached to it. Many organizations which are to some extent self help bodies, such as some of those concerned with mental or physical handicaps, also provide direct voluntary service for their clients. Volunteers assisting in those services are among those whose work is described later in this report.

Pressure Groups

27   We have referred briefly to the work done by volunteers in pioneering the provision of new services. This is closely related to another role, namely that of voluntary effort designed to draw attention to unmet needs and to press for effective action to meet them. A number of organizations whose function

has been and continues to be in the field of social service now recognize a responsibility to involve the public in seeing where action is needed and bringing pressure to bear upon the authorities to make more adequate provision. For example, the National Old People's Welfare Council, the Central Council for the Disabled and the Pre-School Play-groups Association, both nationally and locally, and Councils of Social Service at the local level increasingly fulfil this dual function, using volunteers not only to provide service but also to obtain information and assess, in different ways, the needs of the communities they serve.

28   There are also more recently established groups whose primary function is to publicize needs and to press for action. The Child Poverty Action Group, the Disablement Income Group, and Shelter are now well in the public mind as organizations that exert political pressure for reform. The Disablement Income Group also has a strong self help element, and by circulating newsletters and literature gives its members a sense of involvement, important in helping to overcome the isolation brought on by disability. Local groups raise funds and help individuals both directly and by negotiation with local authorities, and carry out research projects about disability. Pressure groups such as these can be seen as part of the spearhead of the voluntary movement and also have a parallel in the great individual pioneers of the past. This aspect of their work is recognized in the Seebohm Report, and we welcome the statement (para. 495):

'Voluntary organizations pioneered social service reform in the past and we see them playing a major role in developing citizen participation, in revealing new needs and in exposing shortcomings in the services.'

Trade Unions

29   Trade unions are perhaps unique in combining different functions which relate to meeting social needs. Although their primary function is of a different order from that of the voluntary social service organizations, we think it right to include

some reference to them in this chapter. They are primarily self help organizations to assist employees to co-ordinate their efforts in matters which relate to their employment. The major role of unions is to enable their members to have some say in determining the terms of their employment, the nature of their working arrangements and the state of their working environment. They have sought to achieve these objectives by making agreements with their employers that regulate such matters. In this respect, trade unions are perhaps the prime examples of self help organizations. Trade unions have also become concerned with the provision of social services, both as pressure groups and through having representatives on statutory bodies responsible for the administration of these services. In addition, union representatives undertake counselling services to their members at their place of work, which are akin to those undertaken by volunteers concerned with providing personal services in other settings. We know that we must not push these comparisons too far: nevertheless we believe that further study of the role of trade unions in relation to voluntary work could be rewarding.

Community Work

30   *Community Work and Social Change: a Report on Training*, prepared by a Working Party set up by the Calouste Gulbenkian Foundation, was published at the end of 1968. The Working Party concentrated on the training of social workers for this field and left the implications for the training of voluntary workers to our Committee. The Report inevitably reflects a stage of exploration, growth and uncertainty, and it is still difficult in this field to differentiate the role of the volunteer from that of the involved citizen. It is clear, however, that any general development of community work in this country could have a profound effect on the way in which social services are provided, used, recognized and extended. If, therefore, we refer to 'community work' as a significant element in the background to voluntary work, it is because we believe this will prove to be so, not because we claim to understand the full implications of this still somewhat imprecise term. A more general inclusion of the

study of this subject in courses of training for social workers, of which there are already signs, will undoubtedly lead to closer understanding of its contribution and of the elements of which it is composed.

The Churches

31   Although we have refrained from discussing the historical role of the Churches in the field of social service, we would like to refer here to new opportunities which seem now to be opening out for their members in this field. A number of recent reports on allied topics have included non-specific references to the Churches as sources of manpower, as innovators and as providers of resources. We do not disagree with these suggestions but we are aware that religious bodies of all denominations are increasingly finding themselves challenged to define what might be their special contribution to meeting human need of all kinds, whether at national or local level. A report by the Board for Social Responsibility (presented to the Church Assembly in February 1969) examined the Anglican Church's concern for the social services and in particular the exercise by the clergy of their pastoral responsibilities in this field. We were particularly glad to know that the British Council of Churches, in commending the Seebohm, Gulbenkian and Church Assembly reports for study, went on to express the hope

'that special attention will be given to the important implications of the reports, including first, their significance for patterns of local church life, the role of the Church in the changing structures of our welfare society and the contribution which professional social workers may expect from the Churches; and secondly, the role of paid and unpaid non-professional workers in various forms of social service with voluntary and statutory bodies, their preparation for it and their relationship to full-time professionally trained social workers.'

The Future

32   We can imagine that eventually much of the work done by organizations which draw on the help of volunteers from

outside their own areas may be undertaken by local groupings which involve residents in whatever action is needed. This is a long-term, but realistic expectation. It has similar implications for the social services as the expectation of having a fully educated electorate or a working population embarrassed by a superabundance of leisure: and it may be nearer fulfilment than either of these. It is not so near, however, that we can be excused from regarding the present position as the challenge that we have to try to meet. In the chapters that follow, therefore, though we are not unmindful of the shadowy future, we endeavour to deal with current issues as we see them.

Chapter 3
THE VOLUNTEER

33   We decided that as a first step in our enquiry we should
seek to obtain information about voluntary workers, not only
from organizations using them, but also from the volunteers
themselves. We wanted to find out directly from people engaged
in voluntary work how they had come to embark on it, their
motives for undertaking it, the satisfactions or frustrations
which they experienced, and in general how they saw themselves
and their contribution to the social services. The direct approach
to volunteers would, it was thought, also produce further
valuable evidence about people who undertake voluntary work,
in terms of age, sex, social class and occupation, and about the
range and scope of their activities.

Sources of Information

34   We were fortunate, as mentioned in Chapter 1, in being
able to make use of certain studies having a direct bearing on this
aspect of our enquiry. These included a survey of voluntary
workers in Manchester, a study of workers in voluntary organizations in Liverpool; surveys of random samples of the population,
carried out in Portsmouth and Nottingham, and designed to
show to what extent members of the general public were involved in voluntary work; and the report by King Edward's
Hospital Fund for London on Organizers of Voluntary Services in Hospitals.

35   The Committee also planned and commissioned a special
enquiry which was undertaken by the Institute of Community
Studies, and comprised a detailed study of 114 volunteers
working in local branches of six national organizations. The

number of voluntary workers concerned was small, but this made it possible to obtain more detailed and comprehensive information about individual volunteers than was attempted in the other and larger-scale studies which have been mentioned; and it proved extremely illuminating. Finally, members of the Committee themselves interviewed groups of volunteers from various services. A total of sixty-six volunteers from eight different fields of work took part in these group meetings, and, in addition, a small number were interviewed individually on behalf of the Committee. Particulars of these various studies, and of the organizations and types of work represented by the volunteers who were interviewed, are given in Appendix III.

36   In all, close on 800 volunteers gave first-hand information about themselves and their work and, although this is only a minute fraction of the total number of men and women engaged in voluntary work, and is in no scientific sense a sample of that total, this information could not fail to give a more informed understanding of voluntary workers, the actual people with whom we are concerned, than we could otherwise have had.

Who are the Volunteers?

37   The answer to the question 'What sort of people are voluntary workers?' is, without any doubt, that they include people of all sorts. It still seems to be a commonly held view that the typical voluntary worker is a middle-aged, middle-class, married woman. Our evidence suggests that there is some foundation for this belief, but shows also that such people no longer constitute an overwhelming majority among the total volunteer force. Men are playing a much greater part than is sometimes realized. The Liverpool survey found that 'Women do not greatly predominate, neither married nor single women being found in the overwhelming proportions that a "man in the street" view of volunteers would expect'. Portsmouth found that among those claiming to be doing voluntary work the balance of the sexes was practically equal, and the Nottingham study found a similar distribution among those who were doing or had at some time done voluntary work. The Manchester survey

showed that among 10,000 volunteers in Manchester women outnumbered men in the proportion of about three to one, and the report of King Edward's Hospital Fund gave the proportion of men among the total volunteer force of a hospital as anything from an eighth to a third. In the survey carried out by the Institute of Community Studies, 75 per cent of the volunteers interviewed were women.

38   As regards the social class of volunteers, the commonly held view appears to be closer to reality. Almost all the studies concluded that volunteers were more likely to come from the upper occupational groups, and to be better educated, and probably better off, than the average citizen. Almost three-quarters of the volunteers interviewed in the study carried out by the Institute of Community Studies came from the professional and managerial classes. Only two came from semi-skilled or unskilled backgrounds; 47 per cent of the men and 12 per cent of the women had been to universities, and about 75 per cent of both men and women had continued full-time education to the age of 16 or over. Of the volunteers included in this survey (twenty-eight men and eighty-six women) three-quarters of the men and a quarter of the women were in full-time work, thirteen were retired and four were students. In the Liverpool survey 28 per cent of voluntary workers said that their family income exceeded £2000. The report by King Edward's Hospital Fund states that 'all occupations and social classes were represented among the volunteers', but reference to the list of occupations in the Appendix to the report suggests that, although this statement is true, the balance is decidedly towards non-manual workers. Members of the groups of volunteers who were interviewed were found to be predominantly people of good education and middle-class background.

39   Students of the Birmingham College of Commerce carried out an interesting small study to ascertain the amount of voluntary service undertaken by residents in three blocks of flats, described as:

(a) a new block of Council flats in a re-development area;

34

(b) a private block of moderately priced flats on the outskirts of Birmingham;

(c) a new block of flats in one of the best residential areas of the city.

They obtained the following information:

	(a)	(b)	(c)	Total
Total number of households	90	18	67	175
Number responding to the enquiry	82	15	47	144
Individuals aged 15 and over on whom information was given	171	17	97	285
Number helping friends or relatives privately	34	10	13	57
Number engaged in organized voluntary work	8	1	25	34

We have no way of knowing whether these figures are typical, but it is interesting to note the number of people found to be giving help to friends and neighbours privately. They form 20 per cent of the total: the highest proportion, nearly 60 per cent, were in the moderately priced flats (though the number is so small that this may not be significant), and the lowest in the 'good residential' area. The latter has, however, very much the highest proportion engaged in organized voluntary work, nearly 26 per cent compared with 5 per cent and 6 per cent in the other groups. These figures support the view that voluntary work in the sense in which we are using the term is at present a mainly middle-class activity, but also provide one of many indications that willingness to help other people exists and is translated into action at all levels of society.

40 We have found the age range of volunteers to be very wide. Among those interviewed in the survey carried out by the Institute of Community Studies 'the youngest was a schoolgirl of 16, the oldest a single woman of independent means, aged 81', and the hospital survey reported a remarkably similar finding, that the ages of all volunteers in the thirteen hospitals ranged from 14 to 81. Among the volunteers in hospitals the largest number were in their forties and fifties, while the least represented age group appeared to be 25 to 35, 'the age of maximum participation in child rearing and career building'. In both

the Manchester survey and the report by the Institute of Community Studies information was sought about the age and sex distribution of volunteers. The findings show that although the numerical scope of the two studies was very different the age and sex distribution of the volunteers was very similar. The Institute of Community Studies also sub-divided the 'middle-aged' group, and found that 41 per cent of their volunteers were aged between 40 and 60.

Age of Men and Women Volunteers

(Percentage Distribution)

AGE (yrs.)	MEN		WOMEN		MEN AND WOMEN	
	Man-chester Survey	Inst. of Community Studies' Survey	Man-chester Survey	Inst. of Community Studies' Survey	Man-chester Survey	Inst. of Community Studies' Survey
Under 18	12	0	14	1	13	1
18–24	11	11	8	12	9	11
25–59	67	71	64	71	65	71
60 and over	10	18	14	16	13	17
Total	100	100	100	100	100	100
Number of volunteers	1065	28	3466	86	4531	114

41   The growth of voluntary service by the young has already been mentioned, and there are now several organizations with a large and predominantly young membership, though the service given by young people tends, inevitably, to be of short duration. At the other end of the scale there is evidence that in some fields a valuable contribution is being made by people over 60 (three out of forty-seven organizations in Manchester said that among their volunteers this age group was the predominant one), but it seems that at present retired people provide numerically only a minor source of voluntary service. The wide age range of volunteers suggests that voluntary work has an appeal for

people of all ages. In chapter 7 we comment on the effect which certain social changes have had, and are likely to continue to have on the age distribution of volunteers, and the availability of people at different ages for voluntary work. We believe that the recruitment of volunteers in their sixties might be considerably increased if more publicity were given to the help which people of mature years with varied experience could give, and to the wide range of work available to them.

How Many Are There?

42   Any attempt to estimate the total number of people engaged in voluntary work is liable to be misleading for a variety of reasons. Voluntary organizations were asked about their numbers of volunteers. Some did not attempt to give this information, or gave it only for a small number of their branches; the replies which we did receive were not always comparable and were at times difficult to interpret. The difficulty experienced by voluntary bodies in answering this question was accentuated by the fact that a number of them, among these being some of the largest, include in their membership some people who receive payment, and others who are engaged primarily in fund raising, committee work, and other administrative duties, and therefore fall outside the scope of our enquiry. Some of the information which we received does, however, help to give a general idea of the extent of voluntary service at present.

43   We learned that eighteen old people's welfare organizations, out of over 1500 associated with the National Old People's Welfare Council, claimed to have over 26,000 voluntary workers between them; and that five of the constituent bodies of the Standing Conference of National Voluntary Youth Organizations had, between them, over 50,000 voluntary workers. Three of the many branches of the British Red Cross Society had a total of 1550 volunteers, one of them having over 1000; and in 46 branches of the Women's Royal Voluntary Service the total membership was about 14,500: Task Force, operating mainly in London had over 10,000 volunteers. The Department of Education and Science, writing of voluntary part-time youth

workers, said 'their total number is unknown but is probably measured in tens of thousands'. King Edward's Hospital Fund found that in five general hospitals which had started schemes for the use of voluntary workers before 1967 and had appointed organizers there were about 1000 volunteers, and that two psychiatric hospitals each had about 400: there are now many more hospitals with similar schemes, and a great many others which, although they are without organizers, have Leagues of Hospital Friends, often undertaking comparable work. In Manchester it was estimated that well over 10,000 people were giving, on average, two hours a week of their time in a variety of services. The Portsmouth survey suggested that about 10 per cent of the adult population there were engaged in some organized form of voluntary work; and as we have seen a very similar proportion of volunteers was found in the study of three blocks of flats in Birmingham.

44   We should like to emphasize again our awareness that even if we were able to estimate the total number of the volunteers with whom our enquiry is concerned this would represent only part (and possibly a comparatively small part) of the actual voluntary service which is being given. The limitation in the scope of our study does not imply that we attach less value to the work done by those who are not included in it, honorary officers and Committee members, organizers, fund-raisers and office workers, as well as the vast number of those who, unofficially and informally, give help and support to relatives, friends and neighbours, and to the communities in which they live.

The Scope of Voluntary Work

45   Before considering the information which volunteers gave about themselves and their work it may be of interest to touch very briefly on the kinds of work which they do, a subject which will be examined more fully in a later chapter. An enormous variety of work provides opportunities for the exercise of widely differing skills and abilities and for every level of responsibility and initiative. For those of a practical turn, or with

plenty of physical energy, there are jobs like gardening, house decorating and chopping firewood, but there is also a place for those who like to sit quietly sorting files, or to play chess with patients in a psychiatric hospital. Some volunteers undertake the highly skilled and responsible work of counselling and advising people with acute personal problems, others offer a continuing relationship, which sometimes develops into real friendship, to the lonely, the housebound, to offenders and their families. Volunteers may have direct contact with clients of any age, from tiny infants to the very old; or may undertake work in which personal contacts are slight or non-existent, though its purpose is still that of helping other people. There are some organizations, Marriage Guidance Councils, for example, which are highly specialized and seek only volunteers who are able and willing to be trained for and to undertake a particular type of skilled work. Many others cover such a wide variety of duties and kinds of work that almost any volunteer can find an opening in which he can give and receive satisfaction. Some volunteers are attracted by the idea of membership of a uniformed organization, and strong loyalties to the organization itself can develop. Others are repelled by the idea of wearing a uniform and of being organized, but will respond readily to the opportunity of working on their own, with the guidance and support of a professional worker. Some seek work in which they will be associated with people like themselves, others are interested in those who are far out on the very fringes of society. A person who has retired from a demanding professional job may enjoy the continuing mental stimulus of work in a Citizen's Advice Bureau, which requires the volunteer to assimilate and be able to pass on an ever-changing body of knowledge; another will find satisfaction in group activities such as helping in clubs and day centres, while others will welcome the opportunity to acquire new skills and to use them in counselling and supportive services for families.

How People Become Volunteers

46   Volunteers were asked how and why they had originally taken up voluntary work, and their reasons for continuing it.

Their answers showed that many enter voluntary work in the first instance almost by chance, through hearing of it from some friend or relative who is already involved, as a result of a radio or television programme or a written article, or through their church or some other organization. Young people often hear of opportunities for service through their schools or colleges. A minority of the volunteers who were questioned had taken the initiative themselves, and made their own enquiries. We found no evidence of active recruiting methods having been used to any significant extent by individual organizations as a means of bringing in volunteers. The information given by volunteers interviewed in the studies carried out by the Institute of Community Studies and King Edward's Hospital Fund is given in the table below. The first group were asked 'How did you hear of voluntary work for this organization?' (i.e. the organization to which they belonged), and the second 'How did you become a hospital volunteer?' The answers are not entirely comparable, since some of the hospital volunteers said that they had taken up their work through membership of an organization such as the British Red Cross Society or the Women's Royal Voluntary Service, but did not say how they had originally come to join these organizations.

Methods of Introduction to Voluntary Work
(Percentage Distribution)

	METHOD OF INTRODUCTION						
Survey	Personal Contact	Through an Organization	Through Publicity	Own initiative	Through work or school	Total	Number
Institute of Community Studies	42	25	24	9	0	100	114
King Edward's Hospital Fund	29	31	12	15	13	100	86

Answers such as the following are typical:

'A friend of mine mentioned what he did. He didn't press me, but I thought if he could do it I could.'
'A friend said "This is your sort of work, come and help us".'

In short voluntary work at present seems to have an infectious quality and to be something which people catch rather than something which they deliberately seek or which sets out to find them.

The Motives of Voluntary Workers

47   Questions to volunteers about their motives for doing voluntary work were answered generously and frankly. Most commonly the reasons given included an element of altruism, of wanting to help others, but there was also very general recognition of what the volunteer himself was getting from his work: personal benefit, interest, enjoyment, and social contacts. A group of Community Service Volunteers, all of pre-university age, were anxious at first to stress that they were not working from altruistic motives, were not 'do-gooding', and they were not alone in their pejorative use of this term, 'do-gooding'. It was not always clear at first what was meant by it, but it clearly indicates a revulsion from the idea of patronizing benevolence. It seems that the general image of the 'do-gooder' is of someone who, because he believes that he has something to offer which is of benefit to others, regards himself as being superior to the recipients, as offering something from a higher to a lower level, and who enjoys giving service because it feeds his feeling of superiority. He is unaware of what he himself can gain, or that he needs to be equipped with anything but good intentions. This imaginary figure is one with which few volunteers today would wish to be identified. The young volunteers seemed to see their work primarily as a way of gaining knowledge and experience, a step towards maturity, often a break from what they saw as the confines of an over-sheltering home or school background. In discussion, they admitted at a later stage that there was attraction in the idea of helping other people. Indeed,

41

having disposed of any suggestion of 'do-gooding' they were able to admit to a genuine desire to be of service to society.

48   In the study carried out by the Institute of Community Studies the motives mentioned by volunteers were classified as springing from:

(a) Altruism: wanting to do something for others;
(b) Self-interest: seeking personal benefit such as experience, interest, knowledge or occupation:
(c) Sociability: wanting to meet people, to make friends.

A number of informants mentioned a mixture of motives, illustrated by the following replies to questions about their reasons for doing and enjoying voluntary work:

'My own children were growing up and I felt it was time I did something for someone else. I feel everybody should do something.'

'I'd come back from abroad. It sounds rather selfish; I wanted to meet people; I knew no-one here. While doing this I also wanted to do something worth while, but I didn't want too much responsibility.'

'There's always satisfaction to be had in feeling you are helping someone. I suppose, to be honest, almost a selfish satisfaction in giving up some of your time. And there's the opportunity to be in touch with the realities of life—not always possible in a paid profession.'

'I feel very definitely we ought to do something for somebody else. Also it brings you in contact with other people.'

'Partly social reasons—I enjoy meeting people; partly for something to do; and the wish to help other people who need help.'

'There's the satisfaction of meeting a cross section of people; and wanting to help. There's enormous satisfaction in helping people to solve their problems.'

There were also motives which were described in the study as disinterested or rational, for example, 'I can't say I was attracted; I was asked to go into it,' or 'There is obviously a need for this sort of work and I feel I can contribute, therefore I do it.'

Only a few mentioned religious beliefs as their motive for doing voluntary work, but it cannot be assumed from this that such beliefs play only a small part in the motivation of volunteers. Another motive which became evident in the course of these studies was the attraction of belonging to a nationally recognized organization. For some people loyalty to their organization appeared to be a stronger influence than their interest in the particular work which they were doing.

49   Some of these volunteers, then, had undertaken the work because, having heard in some way that help was wanted, they felt that they could give it, and that this would be a reasonable thing to do. Most, however, had felt that voluntary work would meet some need, or combination of needs, of which they were conscious in their own lives, such as the need to do something for other people, or to gain experience of some kind, or to find companionship. There is no reason to deprecate the fact that volunteers do find some of their own needs fulfilled through the work which they do. The same can apply to people following any occupation, whether paid or unpaid, and is dangerous only if the worker's needs are allowed to become paramount, and to submerge those of the people whom the work is intended to benefit.

Satisfactions and Frustrations

50   If voluntary workers are to make their maximum contribution, in terms both of continuity of service and quality of work, they must be helped to enjoy what they are doing, and to see that it is of value. They need to, and for the most part do, find satisfaction in their work, but some inevitably experience some dissatisfaction and frustration. Those whose views were obtained made it clear that on the whole satisfactions outweighed frustrations. The great majority found that the work was rewarding in itself both from the feeling that they were being useful, helping less fortunate people, and contributing to the provision of a beneficial service, and from what they gained in the way of interest, activity, variety of occupation, and social contacts and companionship. Many stressed the sheer enjoyment

which they found in their work. The attitude of a group of workers in clubs for psychiatric patients was that if a club went particularly well they did not think of themselves as having done a good job, but as having had a pleasant and enjoyable evening. A member of the same group said that the personal reward of the workers was a sense of fulfilment, of being a better person: 'Everyone wants to give, and when they give they get something back.' A worker on a London school care committee said at the end of a long discussion about her work, 'I may not have given enough the idea that it is fun. I am grateful to have met the people in the field, and my fellow workers.' A volunteer working with old people said that she had learned a great deal from them; she had been inclined to regret that she had lacked certain advantages, but found that these old people, lacking even more, had acquired wisdom and given it to her. She said 'People should know this about voluntary work, that it is a great compensation and reward.'

51 For some people the main attraction of their voluntary work was its contrast to their normal full-time job or domestic occupation. Work in Citizens' Advice Bureaux, or other services requiring specific knowledge, was appreciated for its mental stimulus; the interest and variety of work with people could compensate for a routine full-time job. The young Community Service Volunteers mentioned the thrill and the surprises which they experienced in learning about people, gaining insight into their ways of life, their problems and how they face them. One said that for a long time he had wondered 'what you were around for at all', but now, for the first time, he felt that he had done something that really mattered. For these young people, as for many other volunteers, spontaneous expressions of appreciation and gratitude from their clients, or the realization that in some particular instance their work had been of real benefit to someone in difficulties were, when they occurred, a great source of satisfaction. Most volunteers, however, regarded this kind of reward as a special bonus and did not depend on it or expect it as a general rule. One said, 'To hear a club member say "I like you" can make you feel on top of the world'; another, after a parent had said how much her child had enjoyed an outing, said,

'If you get such a response nothing else matters.' A volunteer delivering meals on wheels said, 'I get the satisfaction in my particular work from seeing the pleasure it brings; it's as if you were bringing them gold. You can't help feeling it's worth while.' A worker for the Samaritans, who had talked for hours with a man near to despair, and was stopped by him in the street a few days later and thanked for his help, said, 'It made me feel profoundly happy.' A rather different type of satisfaction was that expressed by members of the Simon Community, whose work entailed complete commitment and involvement, identification with the down and out, 'suffering together'. They spoke of the enormous strain of this type of work, but found this in itself to be a satisfaction, as was the feeling that they had 'opted out of the rat-race'.

52   The question of personal involvement was discussed with workers in various services. They were interested in talking about this, and there was a good deal of variety in the views which they expressed. Some thought that some involvement was inevitable where there was any sort of personal relationship, and that a volunteer must give something of himself. Others disagreed, and some went so far as to identify emotional involvement with unsuitability for the work.

53   The frustrations and difficulties which volunteers had experienced in their work fell into three broad categories, concerned with their relationships with professional and other full-time staff, relationships with their clients, and the type of work which they were given to do. Some had found that there were tensions between professional and voluntary workers, particularly in services where their respective roles had not been clearly defined. Of the eighty-six volunteers in hospitals who replied to the questionnaire of King Edward's Hospital Fund, one-fifth expressed some degree of dissatisfaction, and among their comments were 'some staff do not know what a volunteer is for', 'they seem uninterested in me as a person', and 'at first all the staff resented my presence but after a while the barriers broke down'. Only 20 per cent of the volunteers interviewed by the Institute of Community Studies said that they had no frustra-

tions: 13 per cent criticized the inefficiency, inadequacy, or lack of resources of their organizations. Some workers in psychiatric clubs felt that they were not always appreciated by professional staff and some of the Red Cross workers spoke of difficult relationships within hospitals, and lack of liaison between the professionals generally. Some young volunteers working alone regretted their lack of communication with their own headquarters, and their sense of isolation.

54   In relationships with their clients, just as response and appreciation gave great satisfaction, so their absence sometimes caused distress or disappointment. Volunteers working in community care services found that people whom they visited were at times rude or disagreeable, others that their clients were occasionally inconsiderate or took too much for granted. Workers in psychiatric clubs, not surprisingly, found some of their clients 'disturbing': workers for the Simon Community referred to the tragedy of seeing people go down again after they had been helped. Ten per cent of the volunteers interviewed by the Institute of Community Studies were reported to have found that 'personality difficulties of clients' caused them to feel frustrated.

55   Frustrations arising from the work which volunteers were given to do were of two kinds. There were those who found the problems which they faced too difficult for them; and others who felt that not enough was asked of them, and that they had skills to offer which were not being used. In the study carried out by the Institute of Community Studies, 20 per cent of the volunteers said that they found some of the problems which they met to be insoluble, or too difficult. These were, for the most part, people working in services dealing with personal problems or with the giving of advice or information, and it seemed clear that they did not know how to obtain the help which they needed when difficulties came their way. On the other hand there were volunteers in some services who complained that they were never allowed to deal with real difficulties, and that their potential was not being utilized. A volunteer quoted in the Manchester survey said, 'If you have given up half a day it is

soul-destroying just to pass files or arrange the flowers.' It would be unrealistic to expect that frustrations and difficulties in the work of volunteers could be completely eliminated. It does seem, however, that they might be appreciably reduced if more care were given to the selection, preparation and guidance of voluntary workers, if their roles were more clearly defined, and better understood by paid staff, and if all organizations which use them showed more concern for individual volunteers. We have given our attention to all these matters, which are dealt with later in the report.

Attitudes to Their Work and to Paid Workers

56   Volunteers were found to be consistent on the whole in their views about their own work and the special contribution which they could make as volunteers, and also in their some-what unflattering opinions of professional workers. They stressed the freedom, spontaneity, flexibility, and friendliness of volunteers, and contrasted themselves with social workers, whom they tended to see as rigid, inhuman, 'official' in their attitude, and doing their work 'simply as a job'. Only 15 of the 114 volunteers interviewed by the Institute of Community Studies thought that voluntary workers had no advantages over paid workers: 40 per cent saw volunteers as being more flexible, willing, and interested than paid workers; 37 per cent as being more friendly and understanding, and less 'official', and 17 per cent as having more freedom and working under less pressure. Some people gave more than one answer to this question. Their attitudes are expressed in the following examples, taken from many comments of a similar kind on the advantages of voluntary work:

'Quite a number of people regard the paid worker as government appointed. There is a superstitious fear of the professional among lay people.'

'People [helped by volunteers] don't think they are treated like furniture: they like to feel people are doing things because they want to and not because they are paid.'

'The voluntary worker gives a service without seeking reward. The paid worker fulfils an obligation.'

'The voluntary worker is not tied to any form of red tape; the professional worker may be restricted by policy.'

'The voluntary worker can go more as a friend than the paid worker.'

Members of the Committee who took part in discussions with groups of volunteers found very similar attitudes. The friendly unofficialdom of volunteers was stressed as being a quality which enabled them to make easier relationships with clients and to be more readily accepted by them than paid workers. Again, freedom, enthusiasm, and ability to spend more time on individuals, were mentioned as advantages which voluntary workers could offer. A group of workers from a Citizens' Advice Bureau considered that their special contribution was their neutrality, the fact that they were not regarded by the general public as 'them', in the way that officials were. Community Service Volunteers saw themselves as not being in a groove or tied to jobs which were specifically defined, as having no particular label, and therefore able to break new ground and attempt to meet whatever need they encountered. They thought that professionals sometimes had closed minds, were 'inbred', and had lost any desire for exploration.

57   Some of the most illuminating comments were made by volunteers who were interviewed individually on behalf of the Committee. This is how they were quoted by the interviewer:

'He had expected professional social workers to be idealistic and care about what they were doing and be eager to talk about it. He was struck (and so were his friends) by their apathy. They didn't seem to know much about what they were doing. He wondered why they did social work; it just seemed to be a job.'

'There are things a volunteer can do that a professional would not be told about by a client, and would never know about. If you know them in a social way you can do more. Old people are wary of the "men from the Ministry".'

'Volunteers can cut off corners—go on and do things without having to go through channels. Professionals are bound to answer to someone else: I only answer to myself and my conscience. If financial help is needed, by the time the professional does it it is too late: the volunteer can give it and no one else will know about it: there is no record. The old people feel she is an ordinary person, one of them, not someone they are in awe of.'

'The volunteer, going into someone else's home, tries to feel that she is going by virtue of a human contact, and not as part of a statutory service. The humanity of it is the compensation for their shortcomings. In these days of too much administration and growing number of departments it is important to have the element of voluntary work, which is basically a human relationship.'

'It's not the same to be paid. As a volunteer you are in a class on your own: you do it because you want to do it.'

'He has greater freedom of action. The client knows he is doing it because he wants to and because he has some kind of regard for him, and not because it is a paid job.

58   The Institute of Community Studies asked volunteers what they thought were the disadvantages of using volunteers as compared with paid workers. In reply, 34 per cent said there were no disadvantages, 32 per cent that volunteers were less efficient, or had less skill, experience or training, 13 per cent that volunteers were less reliable, 10 per cent that they had less authority or power to help clients, and 9 per cent that they provided less continuity.

59   It will be apparent that the people with whom these volunteers are comparing themselves do not constitute one defined group. In the comments which have been quoted the terms 'professional', 'official', 'paid worker', 'social worker' all appear, and it is probable that in many cases the volunteers were by no means clear what types of worker these particular terms described, or which they were talking about. It can, indeed, be questioned whether some of them had ever encountered the sort of rigid and inhuman official that they believed to be typical. The Institute of Community Studies enquired about the professional social workers with whom the volunteers had contact in their work. Respondents mentioned a great variety of

'professionals', including clergy, doctors, nurses, housing managers, legal advisers, matron of an old people's home, officials of the Ministries of Labour and Social Security, psychiatrists and members of the Women's Royal Voluntary Service. Nearly a fifth of these volunteers said that they had no contact with professional social workers, and about the same number said that they could not answer the question because they did not know enough about the matter to be able to judge.

60   Volunteers who had had more to do with professional workers, particularly in services where their work supplemented that of social workers, sometimes took a rather different view from that of the majority. Members of a group working with disabled people said that they had been pleasantly surprised to find that social workers were human. Workers in clubs for psychiatric patients said that they needed the support of social workers and that it was dangerous for amateurs to attempt professional jobs, though they had found that social workers were not readily available, and were often too busy to give them the guidance they needed. A school care committee worker said she thought that volunteers and social workers had basically the same approach to their work, but that a volunteer could not get near the job a social worker can do in intensive case work, for example with problem families.

61   Nevertheless, the Committee felt that thought must be given to the reasons for the very widespread denigration of officials. One possible explanation is that because, up to the present, so little has been done to clarify the role of voluntary workers, and to recognize their special place in the social services, they have to identify their own contribution and do this by endeavouring to show that paid workers, unlike themselves, have no real feeling for, or interest in their clients. The volunteer who over-identifies himself with his clients may see the social worker, who has to keep statutory boundaries in view, as rigid, tied up in red tape, and as one of 'them', at least partly responsible for his client's difficulties. Other volunteers, in order to convince themselves that their work is worth while, may need to see their clients as 'good' people, and will therefore be critical of

the social worker who, while accepting the client for what he is, and as a person in need of help, does not ignore his inadequacies. The attitudes of social workers and others to volunteers, which will be examined in the next chapter, may, too, have contributed to their own unsatisfactory image. It is possible that the volunteers' idea of the way in which paid workers treat their clients has been coloured by ways in which they themselves feel that they have been regarded and treated by paid workers. It certainly seemed to us, from our discussions with volunteers, that with few exceptions they were getting little help in understanding their own reactions and their relationships with clients and officials.

62   It is possible that the way in which training for social work has developed has some bearing on the apparent difficulties in relationships between social workers and volunteers. In Chapter 9 we discuss ways in which social workers might be helped, through their training, to reach a better understanding of the contribution which voluntary workers can make, and to work more easily with them. At this point we would merely suggest that the influence of psycho-analytic theory on the training of social workers, the emphasis on understanding how personality develops and the effect of earlier experiences on attitudes and behaviour, tended for a time to overshadow the need of some clients for help related to their present environmental difficulties. Problems were defined in such a way that only professional help would be adequate. The struggle for the recognition of social work as a profession has been another factor in the tendency to deny that any effective help could be given by non-professionals. More recent developments in the behavioural sciences, and growing interest in community involvement, are helping to modify these attitudes. Social workers are recognizing more clearly the different kinds of support and help needed by their clients, and are beginning to understand the part which voluntary help might play in meeting some of them. This recognition could, in turn, affect the volunteer's view of social workers.

63   It is suggested in the report of the Institute of Community Studies that volunteers are likely to be as much under an illusion

in thinking that paid workers are just doing a job in which they have no real interest as social workers are who consider that voluntary workers are essentially undependable. We agree with this, and with the further comment: 'Could it be that both views are mainly symptoms of the gulf between the "volunteer" and the "paid worker", and that both will diminish if and when the gulf becomes narrower and each side begins to perceive more realistically the contribution which the other makes?'

Chapter 4

VOLUNTEERS AS OTHERS SEE THEM

64   We received information and opinions about many aspects of the work of volunteers from a number of bodies, central government departments, associations of local authority officers and of social workers, and others. We had asked for their views about the use of voluntary help, its advantages and disadvantages; and it is interesting to compare these views, and those of some of the clients, with the volunteers' image of themselves and their attitudes to paid workers. Many shades of opinion were revealed, but the majority of the bodies engaged in the provision of social services accept the desirability, even the necessity, of using voluntary help. We discovered some anxiety and uncertainty, and areas in which there is distrust or opposition, or where the view of what it would be possible for volunteers to do is so limited as to be almost a negative one. In many fields, however, and most noticeably among some social workers, there is an increasing realization of the positive contribution which volunteers are able to make. It is encouraging to be told in the evidence from the Association of Social Workers that: 'Those members who have already had considerable experience of using volunteers in their work are sure that much can be done to extend their use: others are not so certain.'

Government Departments

65   The attitude of the central government departments with major responsibilities for the personal social services, the Ministry of Health (as it then was) and the Home Office, is one of encouragement and appreciation of the present and future place of voluntary work in these services. The Ministry of

Health points out that though the increasing emphasis on the responsibility of central and local government for the provision of social services is likely to bring about changes in the relationships between paid and voluntary workers, this does not mean that there is any diminution in the need for voluntary help. The Ministry sees the contribution of volunteers as being twofold: 'to complement the work of paid staff, and to provide those services which can more appropriately be given by a volunteer', but also sees it as contributing to the solution of problems of staff shortage. The evidence from the Ministry refers to the need for continual review by voluntary bodies of their objectives and organization, and adds: 'With changing objectives will often go changing individual roles, with consequences for recruitment, management and training.' Of voluntary work in hospitals the Ministry says: 'The services needed are those that can be given most acceptably and therefore effectively by people who can devote time to individual patients, in a way that the best developed medical and nursing services cannot, and who can represent the outside world to patients who are not in touch with their own family or friends.' Reference is also made to the volunteer's need 'to understand the formalities of institutional life and the requirements of the doctors, nurses and others who serve the patient.'

66   The Home Office is interested in the use of voluntary workers in two fields which are at present quite distinct: probation and after-care, and the child care service. The Home Office has stimulated and is actively encouraging a widespread use of voluntary workers in probation and after-care, while emphasizing that although voluntary help can usefully supplement the professional service, it is no substitute for it, and neither could nor should be expected to make good any shortage of probation officers. In a circular issued in November 1965, on the use of voluntary workers, it was suggested that a volunteer may be able to establish a good relationship with an offender who would shun all contact with officials. Mention was made in this circular of various other ways in which volunteers could be of assistance in work with offenders and their families. The probation officer's responsibility for the work done by a volun-

teer was stressed, as was the need for the volunteer to maintain close contact with the probation officer to whom he is responsible.

67 In their evidence on the use of volunteers in the child care service the Home Office refer to ways in which voluntary help is already being used. They mention assistance given in children's homes and other residential establishments, provision of transport, holiday camps and play centres, and some supportive and counselling work for families in difficulties. Of the last they say 'It cannot be too strongly emphasised that careful selection and adequate preparation and support are essential to the success of such schemes.' The evidence continues: 'There is scope for a steady increase within the child care service of all the types of voluntary activity described, subject, of course, to the necessary safeguards.' Dangers which are mentioned in the use of volunteers in the child care service include the risk of masking staff shortages by using voluntary help, and the additional strain and burden which the allocation, preparation and guidance of volunteers might place on over-pressed staff. There is also a reference to what may be a special hazard in this field, the emotional appeal which work with or for children has for many people, including some who, consciously or unconsciously, are seeking only the satisfaction of their own needs.

68 Two other Government Departments, the former Ministry of Social Security and the Department of Education and Science, submitted evidence to the Committee. The Ministry of Social Security referred with appreciation to the invaluable contribution made by members of their war pensions committees, all of whom, in addition to their committee work, undertake visits to the homes of pensioners. They are helped in their work, particularly in rural districts, by other voluntary workers. During the year 1965 over 22,000 visits were paid to the severely disabled and to elderly war widows.

69 The Department of Education and Science is concerned with the work of volunteers in the youth service, in special educational services, in ordinary schools and in play groups of

various kinds. Part time youth leaders, most of whom are volunteers, are described as 'the backbone of the youth service'. Great importance is attached to the training of these workers, and to the encouragement of vitality and variety in training, and the avoidance of over-standardization. The Department has no systematic information about the extent to which education authorities and others make use of volunteers in special services, but considers that handicapped children need much individual attention, both at school and at home, and that for this reason voluntary effort is likely to have much to contribute to these services. They add: 'It is, however, important that voluntary work shall be reliable and practical, and carry no hint of condescension or pity, and that the voluntary workers should accept a place in the "team" and be willing to work under supervision.'

70   The major source of voluntary help in schools is from parents of the children, and this help, which has increased considerably in the last few years, covers a wide range of activities. Some of this effort, in play groups as well as in schools, is directed by parents to helping their own children and thus comes outside the field of voluntary work which we are considering. Much of it, however, is of benefit to the community, and some of these activities are described later, in paragraph 106. There is also particular mention of various types of work with immigrant children, both in and out of school. Another aspect of voluntary work in schools is the participation by school children in community service as an educational subject. The emphasis here is primarily on the benefit to the school children, and we shall have more to say on this subject in Chapter 8 (paragraphs 211 to 214).

71   Broadly it can be said that central Departments with varying emphasis welcome the contribution which voluntary workers can make. They are, generally speaking, uncertain about what this means in terms of precise function, and tend in their evidence to mix comments on the work of voluntary organizations with what they have to say about volunteers. They all, in their different ways, indicate that they will welcome

the views of the Committee as a guide to future policy in this field. The ways in which they are at present giving their support to voluntary work include the making of direct grants from central funds, as to the Young Volunteer Force Foundation, encouraging local authorities to give grants to organizations providing voluntary help, and approving the employment of organizers of voluntary services in hospitals and the refund of expenses to individual volunteers.

Local Authority Officers

72   The views expressed by the associations of chief officers of those local authority departments responsible for social services indicated that comparatively little thought had so far been given by these groups to extending the use made of volunteers or increasing its scope. One association went so far as to state categorically: 'There are few new fields in which it is considered that volunteers could be usefully employed.' Members of these groups tended to see volunteers as useful for only a limited range of activities, and in answer to the question how they saw the advantages of using volunteers there was a good deal of emphasis on economy and on relieving qualified staff of routine or unskilled work. It was also mentioned that volunteers could be helpful at times when paid staff would be off duty; or when large numbers of workers were required for short periods, for example in serving a midday meal. Local authority officers were not, however, unaware of more positive aspects. They referred to the acceptability to clients of the informal and unofficial relationship offered by volunteers, and to the fact that the use of voluntary workers increases the involvement of the community in social problems, and can be seen by clients as an indication of the community's care for them.

73   On the other hand, the evidence from these bodies states clearly what they see as the disadvantages of voluntary workers. Unreliability is the failing most often mentioned, together with a tendency to lose interest and enthusiasm. Some are thought to be unwilling 'to undertake menial but important tasks', or to be willing to work only with clients who are appreciative, or

whom they see as deserving. The volunteers' lack of skill and knowledge, the fear that they may not respect confidence, and their 'need for close but sympathetic guidance and support' are also mentioned as disadvantages. These, however, are difficulties which it should be possible largely to overcome, and should be taken rather as pointers towards measures by which the services of volunteers could be made more rewarding to their clients and themselves. This evidence was given before the publication of the Seebohm Report and there are indications that since then, local authority officers are giving greater consideration to the idea of using volunteers in new ways, and recruiting them directly for work with their staff.

Social Workers

74   Professional associations of social workers, both in their written evidence and in discussions, showed readiness to accept the principle of making increasing use of volunteers, together with an understandable apprehension about its implications. One senior social worker who gave verbal evidence said that the use of volunteers had 'become surprisingly acceptable in the probation service over the past three years'. Later, when asked about the effect on the work of probation officers of using volunteers this officer said it made their work 'harder and more demanding', because of the effort involved in recruiting and supporting voluntary workers. Most of the associations referred in their evidence to the amount of time and thought which need to be given to the selection, recruitment, preparation and guidance of volunteers, and the problem which this presents to busy staff; and to the fact that most social workers would find it impossible to combine this with the day-to-day demands of a normal job. Some social workers tend to retreat from the problem, as do the members of one association who say they 'would not at present be prepared to extend the use of volunteers because the resources deployed in management, recruitment, training and feed-back would not repay the investment'. Others refer to it rather desperately: 'the feeling was that voluntary workers could be very useful if only we had time to cope with them: the conclusion was that it is a vicious circle—we have not

time to organise volunteers so we run around doing the work ourselves'. A more constructive line is taken by another association, which says: 'If recruitment, selection, training and supervision of voluntary workers were to be greatly developed and extended this could provide a valuable arm to the already overloaded social services. But there would need to be at least one professional social worker in every setting where the development was wanted, who had time to devote to this work, and the provision of the means to support it.' Two associations mentioned the danger that social work might become too much a professional concern, and saw the use of voluntary workers as a safeguard against this. They said:

'Voluntary workers should be seen as part of an overall social work plan, not as a stop-gap for lack of trained workers. They are the manifestation of the total community's care for the "socially disabled". They keep the concern alive in the community so that it does not become solely the province of professional workers.' and:

'There is now a danger of the social services becoming over-professionalised and remote from the public they were designed to serve. Imagination is required in seeking new ways of involving the community in the social services, the providers and receivers being fundamentally the same body of people. The volunteer represents the community; sometimes a member of the community already involved with a client may be the best person to help him, and his contribution should not be belittled because he has no official appointment.'

75   In addition to the difficulty of finding the necessary staff time, members of these associations mentioned some of the usual misgivings about voluntary workers, namely fear of their unreliability, of improper use of confidential information, and of failure to appreciate their own limitations. It was thought that lack of skill and knowledge might lead to over-involvement or failure to recognize needs. One association said: 'members find it difficult to see how volunteers can contribute in a casework situation': others commented 'they offer advice which they are not trained to give': and, 'she tended to do too much advis-

ing and counselling herself'. It was thought that some volunteers lacked a sense of responsibility, failed to understand the need for continuity, or would always give their personal affairs priority over the work which they had undertaken.

76   On the other hand, all the professional associations considered that the use of voluntary workers had many advantages. Several mentioned the possibility that volunteers might relieve the pressure on social workers and save their time: but one, whose members have probably more experience than most of using volunteers for work with individual clients, in close association with social workers, said 'it appears to be the general experience that the use of volunteers does not save time but enables the probation service to offer a better and fuller service to some of its clients'. One of the advantages most frequently mentioned was that volunteers, not being under pressure, as social workers are, to fulfil statutory obligations, can spend more time on individual clients or families or can more easily maintain a long-term interest in lonely or isolated persons. Social workers, like their administrative colleagues, also value the increased involvement of the community which is brought about by the use of voluntary workers. They mention too, that for some clients volunteers are more acceptable than paid workers, because they are not associated with authority, with the law, or with hospitals and the treatment of mental or physical illness.

77   It seemed from the evidence that most of the associations of social workers had based their replies on the views of a comparatively small proportion of their membership; and it is possible, therefore, that they are not at present representative of the whole body of members, or even of the majority. It is likely, however, that these views are those held by the more forward-looking members of their respective associations, and can be taken as representing a significant trend of opinion.

Those Who Receive the Services

78   The personal social services, though of benefit to society generally, exist primarily for their clients. The reactions of

clients to voluntary workers are therefore of central importance. This is an area which justifies much more comprehensive study, but the Committee has had to content itself with some very limited investigations, designed to discover something about the relationships between volunteers and clients. Small studies were carried out for the Committee in which members of clubs run by volunteers, people receiving visits from volunteers in their own homes, young people in residential institutions for delinquents, and patients in hospitals using voluntary workers, were interviewed. The interviews were carried out by Rose Deakin, who saw a small number of people who were visited in their own homes by volunteers (old people, former patients of psychiatric hospitals, and disabled people); and also members of three clubs run by volunteers: by Michael Power, who interviewed boys in a Borstal Institution visited by students from a theological college and by undergraduates, and in an approved school visited by other volunteers: and by Jan de Rocha who saw patients in six hospitals where voluntary workers were used.

79   These interviews showed that the clients' opinions of volunteers were generally favourable; but on the whole the impact made by volunteers who were visiting people in their own homes was surprisingly small. Reactions were vague and confused, particularly among the old people, some of whom denied that they had received any visits at all. One old lady said that she had had a visitor who came three times a week for an hour and used to sit and talk to her, but she did not know her very well and did not know why she came. She later added that she had had another visitor who 'was very nice and always brought something'. In most of the interviews with old people it was impossible to estimate the quality of the relationships between them and the volunteers. There were only two definitely hostile reactions, both from old people, and both related specifically to young volunteers. In contrast, several of the clients particularly appreciated the visits which they had had from young people, enjoyed seeing them, found them easy to talk to, and were pleased with their willingness to give practical help of various kinds. One old lady who said that she would not ask the boys who visited her for anything she wanted because 'you

don't like to make yourself too cheap to young gentlemen', later revealed that the young gentlemen chopped firewood, brought in the coal and cleaned windows for her. Three of the old people said that they would not want visits from people of their own age.

80   The other two groups seemed much less vague about their visitors, and the psychiatric patients in particular expressed real appreciation of the help which they had received. The visits to them were organized by mental health associations, the aim being to offer friendship. This concept raises some difficulties, since friendship is often not the relationship which the client wants or the volunteer is able to give, yet two of these psychiatric patients seemed to regard their visitors as friends in the true sense of the word. Both were lonely women who had felt cut off from the community; their visitors had invited them to their own homes, and were helping them to find useful occupation, one in part-time employment and the other in voluntary work. They had become much more relaxed in their contacts with other people, and felt that this was largely due to the help of the voluntary workers. Another of these patients spoke warmly of her voluntary visitor, as a person who had treated her with understanding but not with pity, who had helped her to overcome her fear of going out or of meeting people, and had made her feel useful. In general this group of clients were fully aware of the nature of the organization helping them, and did not depend on their visitors as friends, although they felt a degree of friendship and accepted help offered in a friendly way.

81   The disabled people who were interviewed had on the whole received less help from voluntary visitors, and some of them would have liked more. One, well educated, thoughtful and articulate, gave a very detailed and sensitive account of her experience with voluntary visitors. She was not unduly critical but had found difficulty in coping with the attentions of visitors, paid as well as voluntary, who wished to give her services which she did not want. She said of one elderly volunteer that she 'told all the news, gossiped on and was useful in one sense', but

added: 'I'm a captive audience, I have to adapt myself to her.' She found it a strain to adapt, to listen to chatter and be 'cheered up', and was always exhausted when her visitor left. She also found it irksome that gratitude was expected from her, but added that paid workers seemed to expect it just as much.

82   Members of clubs run by volunteers felt that they benefited in a variety of ways from their attendance. In an old people's club the members appeared to have very little contact with the voluntary workers who ran it, but the same group of members always sat together, and most of them were content, or even preferred, simply to sit and chat. Some also attended other clubs where activities such as basket work and singing were arranged. In the club for psychiatric patients there was deliberately as little distinction as possible between members and helpers. Each helper tried to befriend certain members, both in the club and outside, and the members took a considerable part in the running of the club. Members felt that they were helped by being able to feel useful in the club, and for some of them attendance at the club was clearly an important feature of their lives. For the physically handicapped the club provided social contacts for some people whose opportunities for getting out and meeting people were otherwise extremely limited. There was appreciation of this, and also of the service which the club provided for obtaining books from the public library for its members. This club had a well organized voluntary transport system, as did the club for psychiatric patients.

83   The Borstal and approved school boys all valued their contact with the volunteers who visited and stayed in the institution in which they were living. The major advantage in the eyes of both groups was that the volunteers were people 'from outside': they represented contact with the outside world and helped to keep things in proportion. The fact that the volunteers were young, near in age to some of the boys, was also appreciated. All the boys were fairly definite that, whilst they had welcomed the volunteers and made good relationships with them, they were not in their sense of the word 'mates'. They enjoyed the relationship but recognized that it was not of their own choice,

but was provided for them in a particular setting and for some particular purpose. The Borstal boys were clearer than those in the approved school about the purpose of the visits, and saw the volunteers as individuals making a special contribution. This was partly because these boys were older, more intelligent, and more articulate than those in the approved school; but also because in the Borstal Institution the volunteers were used in a planned and directed way, while in the approved school they were seen as part of a stream of visitors who were encouraged to come in informally and mix with the boys.

84   The group of hospital patients who were interviewed saw volunteers primarily as people who were helpful in undertaking practical tasks. Two-thirds of these patients were quite sure that shortage of staff was the main reason for using volunteers. They did, however, see other advantages, several of them saying that the great thing about volunteers was that they were people like themselves, from outside, and therefore they could talk to them and exchange gossip as they would not feel free to do with a nurse or other member of the staff. They thought that volunteers could take a special interest in patients without friends or relatives to visit them.

85   Although we have quoted some comments which seem critical of voluntary workers we should not wish to give the impression that we regard these criticisms as typical. We recognize the great value of the work which is being done by very many volunteers who visit people in their own homes and else-where; and we believe that there are many lonely people not at present receiving visits who would welcome them. We believe too that volunteers have a particularly important role in visiting, as representatives of the outside world, those who for one reason or another are living in any kind of institution. We have mentioned that the Borstal boys, and those in the approved school, did not regard their voluntary visitors as 'mates'; but another Borstal boy asked for a voluntary associate because he wanted a visitor who was 'not an official of any sort', and who would 'sit on my side of the table'. In such a case, after the in-troductory visit, the Borstal boy would have to take the initiative

in obtaining a visiting order to send to his associate: this emphasizes the unofficial nature of the visit and the fact that it is within the control of the boy himself—an important consideration.

86   These small studies of the attitudes of clients have been particularly valuable in illustrating the importance of giving purpose and direction to the work of volunteers; and showing how much less effective it is if it lacks a definite aim which is understood by both worker and client. Those who said they did not know why volunteers visited them, or denied that they ever did, were able to understand and appreciate the functions of other people who came to their homes, such as the home help and the district nurse, and spoke warmly of them. Some thought that volunteers visited them because of some need which they themselves felt, that the visitor was lonely or needed something to do: and it may be that this impression was deliberately fostered by some workers in order to diminish the sense of obligation felt by the client. This approach can hardly be helpful in the introductory stages, when the service which is being offered needs to be not only understood by the worker, but also acceptable to the client. Most of the people interviewed clearly appreciated help of a practical kind, and there were others for whom it seemed that such help would have been welcome if it had been offered. An old man who denied having a visitor and said that he did not want one, was found to be very lonely, and said that he was depressed and felt that no one cared. His wife was in hospital and he was struggling with long journeys to visit her. The investigator had the impression that help offered in a practical way with transport could have been used also for support and companionship. We believe that almost all visiting could become more helpful and more welcome if volunteers were given greater opportunities of learning about the needs of the people they visit; and about ways of overcoming the barrier of unresponsiveness which they often meet initially, particularly in old people. An initial personal introduction by someone already known to the client can be very helpful.

87   Another point which emerged clearly was the importance of regularity and reliability to people receiving a service.

Several referred to the number of haphazard visitors with whom they had had contact; and one in particular expressed a wish for a regular and constant visitor in whom she could confide and have confidence. Another comment was: 'It's all very well, these people, you are frightfully pleased to see them but they come and go, they are ships in the night.' One organization which was asked about the frequency and regularity of the visits paid by its workers said that it was difficult to keep a check on this. It was believed that all visitors were in contact with their clients, but that some were probably not visiting very frequently.

88   In general the clients who were interviewed seemed well aware of the contribution which voluntary workers can make. The fact that they were not all equally appreciative of the help which they received was not necessarily the fault of the volunteers. It may illustrate the unevenness of much of the work done by volunteers at present, but does not conceal its potential value. This is most clearly seen in the comments of the psychiatric patients, some of whom felt the help which they had received in re-establishing contacts in the community to be invaluable.

Conclusions

89   The attitudes which have been described in this chapter support the view that the need for increased knowledge and understanding between volunteers and officials of all kinds is mutual. In general, the more people know about the work which can be done by volunteers, when it is properly organized and appropriately used, the more they value it: this applies equally to those who represent bodies which are responsible for providing services, social workers who take part in them, and clients who benefit from them.

90   From the evidence which has been given by central government departments we conclude that they are seriously interested in seeing considerable development in the use of volunteers. They are aware of the dangers of over-dependence on voluntary help; but in our view they could do a good deal more than has been done at present to provide the active support

and help which are necessary in order to avoid these dangers. We make some further comments and suggestions on this point in Chapter 10.

91   The restricted view which some local authority officers seem to take of voluntary help may be due to the fact that many of them, at the time when they were preparing evidence for this Committee, had little direct experience of the work of volunteers. It is possible too, that the tendency of certain members of some authorities to wish to undertake detailed work which is properly the function of staff, and possibly of professional staff, has contributed to doubts about the desirability of using voluntary help. This difficulty seems to be decreasing, and recommendations made in the Report of the Maud Committee on the Management of Local Government have assisted the process. At the same time, increasing general interest in and awareness of the additional resources which volunteers can offer are affecting the attitude of local authorities. Since we were appointed we have seen many signs of their growing recognition of the help that volunteers can give and of readiness to make use of it.

92   Social workers face a rather different problem. There may be some who are still concerned about the impact on their professional standing of permitting lay people to take part in their work; and more who are anxious about the harm which might be done to clients by unskilful workers. For the most part, however, their anxieties relate to the difficulty of finding the time and manpower required to make effective use of volunteers. It is not surprising that some see this difficulty as being almost insuperable. Many of them realize that the main object of bringing in volunteers is not to relieve the paid staff but to improve the service, to enrich its quality and extend its scope. In order to achieve this, people must be available to spend time with volunteers, to recruit and select them, to plan and organize their training and their work, and to provide consultation or advice when required. Volunteers themselves may be able to assist in these functions, but the use of some paid staff is inescapable. Where volunteers are helping in casework services a

fairly high proportion of professional staff will be needed to work with them: the ratio of one social worker to about ten volunteers has been mentioned. It has been found, too, that the increased coverage made possible by the use of voluntary help often results in new needs being brought to light, and thus in additional work for professional staff. These anxieties are likely to continue to colour the attitude of social workers to a much increased use of voluntary help, until they can feel confident that the implications are understood by their employing bodies. We also see a need for social workers to be more aware of the many functions which voluntary workers can perform, and of the potentialities of a partnership between volunteers and professional staff.

Chapter 5

WHAT VOLUNTARY WORKERS DO

93　　We have already referred to the very wide range of tasks and types of work which voluntary workers are undertaking at the present time. Perhaps the best way to indicate the breadth and scope of voluntary work is to classify the jobs which are being done, not according to the services or organizations in which they are undertaken, but according to the type of commitment and the various degrees and kinds of knowledge, skill and understanding required. In making this classification we do not wish to imply that particular types of work are more valuable or praiseworthy than others; but it would be foolish not to recognize that volunteers are needed to work at many different levels, requiring different qualities and different kinds of preparation or training. The classifications suggested below are not clear-cut: there is a good deal of overlapping, and many volunteers may be doing work which comes into more than one category. Broadly, however, the following are the types of work in which volunteers are engaged, excluding those with which, as explained in Chapter 1, we are not directly concerned:

　(i) Work of a mainly practical kind.
　(ii) Work for which special skill or knowledge is required.
　(iii) Work involving personal relationships:
　　　　(a) with individuals and their families;
　　　　(b) in residential settings;
　　　　(c) with groups in other settings;
　　　　(d) with those alienated from society;
　　　　(e) in emergency services.

Work of a Mainly Practical Kind

94　　Many people feel that practical help is the kind of service which they are best fitted to give, and some of them, perhaps the young especially, derive a good deal of enjoyment from work of this kind. Such work may not involve the volunteer in any significant personal relationship with the people helped (though groups of young people working on community projects such as making an adventure playground, or a garden for the blind, or clearing oil from beaches, clearly gain a great deal from the fellowship of their own groups). Some of the work undertaken by volunteers in hospitals falls into this category. In the report *Organizers of Voluntary Services in Hospitals* a list is given of about seventy jobs which, at the time of the survey, were being undertaken by voluntary workers in the ten general and three psychiatric hospitals covered by the survey. They included arranging flowers, answering the telephone, checking linen, tidying magazines, and sorting files, as well as work of a more personal kind. Another type of practical work which may involve little or no personal contact is the provision of transport, as is done for example by the organization known as Community Transport in Birmingham. This organization, providing its own transport and manned by voluntary workers, undertakes to move furniture and equipment, or to take groups of people on holidays or outings. Other examples are the cooking and preparation of meals on wheels, the cleaning and decorating of property for the accommodation of old or homeless people, and the repairing, storage and distribution of clothing.

95   Most work which is mainly of a practical kind does, however, bring the volunteer into direct contact with the people whom he is undertaking to help. In includes help with gardening, shopping or household tasks for old or handicapped people; delivering meals on wheels; transporting people to and from hospitals and clinics; taking parents to visit children who are away from home, or relatives to visit patients in hospital. In hospitals it can include serving meals and beverages; taking a library trolley round the wards; helping to dress and undress patients; escorting patients from one department to another, or taking them in wheel chairs to the hospital chapel. Work of this kind may range from the performance of quite simple tasks of limited duration to work which, starting in a practical way, can

lead to the formation of a long-term, supportive relationship. A volunteer may drive a disabled person to and from work until a motor vehicle is supplied; or may undertake to open up the house of a woman returning from hospital, light the fire and see her settled in, leaving when her husband or another member of the family returns home. We have also some examples of volunteers offering long-term practical help of a very special kind: it was essential for a child suffering from coeliac disease that she should not eat ordinary bread or cakes but should have them made from gluten-free flour: her parents were casual in their attitude and limited in intelligence, but a volunteer was found who, having a child of her own suffering from the same condition, made bread and cakes for the other child as well as for her own each week. A somewhat similar type of help was given by another volunteer to the mother of three young children, all needing to attend hospital and requiring a special diet: the volunteer accompanied the mother and children to hospital, and helped the mother to understand and cope with the special diet required. Another volunteer went weekly to the home of a woman who was housebound because she had a mentally subnormal son who could not work or use public transport: the volunteer stayed with the son so that the mother could go out, or took both for a drive. Some volunteers offer help to the staff of residential establishments of various kinds, and this, even when the main purpose is the performance of some practical task, usually brings them into touch with the residents. Examples of work which is mainly practical are legion, and many more could have been given. It is usually appreciated by those who benefit from it; and is liked by many voluntary workers because of its immediately visible results and often limited personal involvement. This kind of work merges imperceptibly into the type of work described in paragraph 98.

Work For Which Special Skill or Knowledge is Required

96　Some of the work undertaken calls for special skill or knowledge, which the volunteer may already possess or may need to acquire. Among those who take steps to equip themselves for such work are the many members of the British Red

Cross Society and the St John Ambulance Brigade who, after taking courses in home nursing or first aid, use their knowledge and skill to help the sick or handicapped. They give their services in hospitals, clinics and residential establishments, or to people in their own homes, act as escorts, and attend at public functions. Other volunteers needing special knowledge are those who work with the deaf, who can offer much more if they learn how to communicate with them directly, instead of through an interpreter. Different kinds of skill are required by those who repair and bind books for hospital libraries; who instruct children in road safety; or who offer beauty treatment or hairdressing to people in hospitals or residential homes. Workers in Citizens' Advice Bureaux and other information services, who may receive enquiries about problems of almost any kind, not only need to acquire a considerable amount of information initially, but must be prepared to continue to learn, in order to keep it up to date.

97   People who already have some special skill, knowledge or training and who may be using it in their daily work, often offer to use it also in some form of voluntary service. Among them are those who can act as interpreters for immigrants with language difficulties, or teach them English; and teachers of other subjects, including handicrafts, who hold classes in clubs, offer interests to patients in psychiatric hospitals or assist with occupational therapy. Many doctors, lawyers, accountants, social workers and members of other professions are giving voluntary service by using their specialized knowledge, either occasionally to meet a particular need, or more regularly as advisers to some organization. These are only a few examples from the wide range of skilled voluntary service which is being given.

Work Involving Personal Relationships

(a) With individuals and their families

98   Volunteers may work with individuals and their families by visiting them in their own homes, in residential settings such as hospitals, prisons and homes of various kinds; or sometimes

72

by seeing them in the offices or other premises of the organization concerned. This work can range from skilled counselling to the simple befriending of a lonely or housebound person. We have already suggested, however, that the concept of 'friendly' visiting needs some re-thinking, and we believe that to many workers the term is no longer acceptable. It seems to us that the visitor who just drops in, whether occasionally or regularly, without some real purpose which is understood by the visitor and has been conveyed to and accepted by the client, may achieve little or nothing. Yet there is undoubtedly an important place for the kind of service which can be given by people who, while they are in no sense qualified as social workers, can alleviate loneliness and isolation, demonstrate the concern of society for its less fortunate members, enlist the help of a social worker if required, or call in some appropriate statutory or voluntary service if the need arises. It is also clear that there are enormous resources available, in the way of volunteers willing to undertake such work, though it is doubtful whether anything like the best use of these resources is being made at present.

99   A preliminary study of eighty questionnaires selected from those returned by voluntary organizations showed that in forty-eight of them volunteers undertook visiting; and in nineteen it was their principal activity, over 50 per cent of their volunteers being involved. Twelve, including four of those for whom visiting was the main activity, said that they had no arrangements for the selection of volunteers. The impression gained from these replies was that most of the visitors working for these organizations were doing their work very much alone and unsupported. Sixteen of the forty-eight organizations whose volunteers were engaged in visiting had no arrangements for meetings at which their visitors could discuss their work.

100   It would seem that at present the majority of volunteers undertaking the visiting of people in their own homes are visiting old people; but there are also many doing similar work in other services, and opportunities for such work are continually increasing. Examples can be taken from the report of a

survey carried out in South-east Lancashire and East Cheshire by Jean Thornley, and published in the summer of 1965. In this report over forty voluntary bodies and local authority departments in the area were mentioned as requiring volunteers for home visiting (in addition to many other forms of voluntary work). The people with whom these bodies were concerned, and for whom visitors were wanted, included the old or sick, physically and mentally handicapped people, families in difficulty, invalid children, and people suffering from particular disabilities, the blind, deaf, spastics, diabetics and others. Some organizations said that no qualifications were needed; others that volunteers would have to acquire some knowledge, for example, how to communicate with the deaf blind; and one specified that 'trained women volunteers' were needed. The Lancashire and East Cheshire report made no particlar mention of home visiting in connection with the care of offenders and their families, but the use of voluntary workers in this service has been actively encouraged during the last few years and is steadily increasing. The need for volunteers would have been less publicised in 1965, when the report was published, than it has been since.

101   In some settings volunteers are now playing a significant part in casework and counselling services for individuals and families with special problems, either as ancillary to a professional social work service or as a substitute for it. They may work in close association with social workers, as in the probation and after-care service, and some local authority services, and sometimes in such voluntary organizations as Family Service Units and the Family Welfare Association. The Blackfriars Family Counsellors Project uses specially selected voluntary workers to do the actual visiting and counselling of families with problems: these volunteers are supervised by an experienced social worker who is responsible for selection and training and is always available for consultation and guidance. Yet another pattern is that of the Marriage Guidance Councils in which all the counselling work is carried out by volunteers, the only paid workers being consultants and officials of the National Marriage Guidance Council, which directs policy and is responsible for

the selection and basic training of all counsellors. As a matter of general policy the National Marriage Guidance Council attaches great importance to very careful initial selection of counsellors; and all volunteers are put through lengthy and rigorous selection procedures. It is also national policy that the formal training of counsellors shall be supplemented by their regular attendance at meetings at their local centres, for discussion of their cases with a paid consultant, usually a psychiatrist or a psychiatric social worker. It seems, however, that some centres have not adopted this practice, though all are encouraged to do so.

102   We have been given a very large number of examples of work undertaken by volunteers in services involving casework and have selected the following as illustrating the part which a voluntary worker can play:

(i) A middle-aged manic-depressive woman whose husband had recently had a coronary thrombosis was being visited by both a professional and a voluntary worker. The professional worker was unable to visit to the extent which was necessary during the woman's depressed periods and also believed that his visiting confirmed her fears of mental illness. The voluntary worker was able to visit in the interim and to be helpful with any problems which might arise.

(ii) A young man, in and out of institutions, including children's homes, borstal and prison, was found by the probation officer to be lonely and apathetic. Another young man, a voluntary 'associate' was introduced. Contact was uncertain for some months, but a common interest in bachelor cooking helped to cement a friendship. The associate visited the client when he was briefly in hospital. The client's appearance and self-confidence improved: he found a girl friend, and he has recently married. The associate attended the wedding and the reception was held at his flat. The two men still keep in touch from time to time.

(iii) A married woman, an ex-health visitor, undertook to visit a family known to the Children's Department, who were concerned about the children's lack of proper care. She visited them every morning for an hour, and sometimes longer, after she had taken her two small sons to school. Her methods were very much those of a Family Service Unit worker and a friend. She was able to gain the mother's confidence, and together they washed up, made the beds, planned the day's meals, and indeed established a pattern of housewifery. Through this joint effort a bond was formed which led to discussion of the care of the children and of relationships within the family, and enabled the mother to express her uncertainties, her worries, her joys and her fears. It was time-consuming and needed to be unhurried. There were many ups and downs, and for the child care officer and the children's officer there was anxiety at the beginning as to whether or not the children ought to be removed to a place of safety. After some years (as the children grew older and no more were born), and through many vicissitudes, a more stable pattern was established: the school reports that the children now seem to be well adjusted and better cared for.

(iv) This is a large family with a very disturbed mother, and this particular volunteer's contribution is to make the mother and the family feel that they have somebody who takes a personal interest in them, who takes them out sometimes and who does not mind if the mother is not there when she calls, because she still comes to take the children out. When the mother is there the volunteer talks to her about clothes, or gives her a treat by taking her to a café in the West End of London. The continuity of this relationship has been of great importance to the family because, whereas the mental welfare officer has changed three times, the health visitor twice and the youth employment officer and various other people have come in and gone out, this volunteer has gone on visiting, on a simple, friendly basis. This has enabled the family to feel that their social need is recognized; that they are not regarded as inadequate but as a family which needs a friend. What seems to support them is the fact that the volunteer is there, and continues to be there as a friend would be. It is a mutually satisfying relationship.

(b) Work in residential settings

103   Volunteers undertake work with people in almost every kind of residential setting. In hospitals they visit and talk to lonely patients, read to them, write their letters, or may take them for walks or outings: and much the same type of service is given to people in homes for the old or the handicapped. Some people befriend children in children's homes, visiting them, taking them out and sometimes inviting them for holidays. This is a type of service which is offered by many people, but for which there is less demand now than formerly. One common feature of the various residential establishments in which voluntary workers visit is that the people in them are usually not there by their own choice, but by force of circumstances. Whatever the reason, whether infirmity, misfortune, or because they themselves have offended in some way, they welcome contact with people 'from outside' and the interest which such people show in them; but this kind of contact, like that with people in their own homes, is most likely to be helpful when the visitor initially has some specific purpose or job, through which informal relationships can develop.

(c) Work with groups in other settings

104   Volunteers assist in group activities in a large number of different fields. A notable example is the Youth Service which has always depended to a very large extent on voluntary help. This service, in which the full-time trained youth leaders are assisted by a very much larger number of part-time workers, the majority of whom are voluntary, is primarily concerned with 'the leisure activities of ordinary young people between the ages of 14 and 20'. Volunteers take a leading part in these very varied activities, ranging from the old-established uniformed organizations, through youth clubs of all kinds, to some new and experimental schemes. A fairly recent development of this kind is the work of the Week-enders' Scheme, designed to meet some of the needs of mobile young people, primarily in holiday resorts and at holiday periods when most youth clubs are closed.

These projects, co-ordinated by the National Association of Youth Clubs, and carried out for the most part by young volunteers, provide centres, sometimes open all night, where in an informal and non-authoritarian atmosphere information is available, coffee is served, and bedding may be provided.

105   Volunteers also take part in play and holiday schemes for school children, or for those under school age, initiated and financed either by voluntary bodies or by local authorities. Sometimes individual volunteers assist paid and qualified staff; and sometimes a group of voluntary workers will take over the running of a project entirely. Schemes of this kind may serve a whole neighbourhood, but are sometimes provided for a specially selected group, for example, children of families with whom a Children's Department is actively concerned, who are thought likely to benefit particularly from some group activity in holidays or after school hours. There is scope for work of a similar kind in hospitals, where volunteers play with or read to children who are patients, or run a nursery for the children of mothers attending hospital daily.

106   Another example is the help given in schools, often by parents of the pupils. The headmaster of one primary school which has help of this kind, and where parents have provided a swimming pool, said: 'You can imagine how long it would take to prepare a class of 40 infants for swimming. We have a duty rota of three or four mums coming in every day to undress and afterwards to dry and dress the children before taking them back to the classroom'. In the same school a member of staff spoke of help given in the library, 'helping the children to find their way about, repairing books and cataloguing. The biggest help to me is when I can call upon a mother to take a small group off my hands who happen to be bursting with energy and want to run around. I see no objection to mothers reading stories. They do it at home anyway, and it leaves me free to concentrate upon those most in need of individual attention.'

107   A great deal of work is undertaken by volunteers in clubs of various kinds, for old or physically handicapped people,

the mentally ill, the blind or deaf; and with a variety of special groups; for example, mothers of young children, prisoners' wives, or mentally handicapped children. In some places volunteers also run or assist with day centres or luncheon clubs for old people. Many of the clubs or centres are run entirely by volunteers, who are responsible for the organization, for bringing in new members, and for planning and carrying out appropriate activities, which may include dancing, handicraft or other classes, entertainments and outings. Some volunteers confine themselves mainly to this aspect of the work, the provision of a club with various activities for its members: but others seek to involve the members in the running of the club, to get to know them individually, and to minimize the distinction between members and helpers. Clubs vary, too, in their structure and the degree of formality. One example of a completely informal club is the project called 'Friendship Unlimited', which was started in Nottingham in 1966 by a group representing various social agencies, and is staffed entirely by volunteers. These volunteers run a centre which is open every Sunday evening and on one evening during the week, and caters for lonely or isolated people of any age. During 1967 the average attendance was about thirty per night. The aims are described as follows: 'It is important that there is no club atmosphere, that names and addresses are not taken unless anyone wants to give the information, that the only charge made is for tea or coffee, and that there is no attempt to hold people but only to get them back into the swim of life'. In other places volunteers see the main need of their clients as being a place where they can meet their friends, sit and talk with one another, and have tea. The provision of transport for members is often an important part of the work of volunteers in services of this kind.

(d) Attempts to reach those who are alienated from society

108   There is nothing new in the concept of trying to help people who are in difficulties, and in particular those who are socially unacceptable, by living among them, to some extent sharing their problems and sufferings, accepting them, and offering companionship without any shadow of authoritarianism or moral judgment. Examples of this kind of work can

be found throughout the ages and from all parts of the world, but particular attention seems to have been given to it recently, and the imagination of many people, especially young people, has been fired by the idea of helping those who are 'unattached' or alienated from society in their own country in this way. Some of these projects, such as those carried out by the Simon Community, include the provision of some kind of shelter for people who need somewhere to live but are unable to fit into any organized way of living. Sometimes there is just a place, open day and night, where coffee can be obtained; where companionship is never forced on anyone; where those who prefer it can remain silent or alone; but where there will always be a listener for anyone who wants to talk. Volunteers have pioneered and worked in a number of such projects, of which a recent example was the centre for homeless girls, described in the report *Rootless in the City*. At this centre, young volunteers working in association with the psychiatric social worker who was in charge of the project, were able to make a contribution which was beyond what could be expected of young people, or could have been achieved by a social worker alone. A rather different kind of work is that for drinkers of methylated spirits or people with other types of addiction who are sought out in their own haunts. New movements of this kind are constantly coming to notice, and this work, too, appears to have a particular appeal for the young. Work such as this obviously carries risks for young volunteers, and much of it imposes enormous strains on those who undertake it. This is particularly true of work which entails actually living with 'misfits', and of the close identification and involvement with persons in need which are characteristic of work such as that of the Simon Community. The founder of this Community suggested that two years was the longest period for which anyone should continue to do full time work of that type. In any case, much of the work for people in this category must necessarily be transient, because it is dealing with a mainly shifting population.

109   In the field of delinquency volunteers have an especially important part to play. They demonstrate the continuing concern of the community for those who have alienated themselves

by anti-social behaviour and might be thought by some people to have forfeited their right to be helped. By attempting to bridge the gap between delinquents, who often constitute an annoyance or a threat to society, and ordinary law-abiding citizens, volunteers are performing a creative function. This is work which calls for considerable resilience in the face of disappointment, for maturity of judgment, and for personal convictions which are likely to remain unaffected by the superficial attractions of the delinquent way of life.

(e) Work in emergency services

110   Among the volunteers who undertake to help in emergencies are those who risk their lives to save others who are in danger, as members of mountain search and rescue teams, or as volunteer life guards on bathing beaches. The Samaritans offer a service, manned continuously by volunteers, to persons who are in a state of acute personal distress, which may lead them to contemplate suicide: such persons can telephone a member at any time and will be offered advice, support or comfort. Members of the Volunteer Emergency Service, providing their own transport, undertake urgent errands, such as carrying supplies of blood or of vaccine, at the request of hospitals. Other volunteers help in emergencies of a more domestic kind, and this service, among others, is offered by members of some of the 'Good Neighbour' and similar schemes which have been set up by churches in various parts of the country. Through these schemes any member of the parish who is faced with a domestic crisis and is in urgent need can obtain help such as might be given by a good neighbour until the difficulty is resolved or the appropriate service can be brought in. Mention must be made here of voluntary work done, notably by members of the Women's Voluntary Service (as it then was) in all the war-time services coming under the broad heading of Civil Defence, and of the help available now in any major emergency or disaster from members of certain national and local organizations. These include established bodies, notably the British Red Cross Society, the St John Ambulance Brigade, and the Women's Royal Voluntary Service; and also a new service, the Voluntary Civil Aid Service, set up after the disbandment of the

Civil Defence Corps in 1968. Former member of the Corps have formed local groups in a number of areas to provide a trained volunteer force which could assist the authorities in the event of emergency.

Popular and Unpopular Tasks

111   One of the questions which voluntary organizations were asked was what kinds of work they found to be popular or unpopular with their volunteers, and what they thought were the reasons for their likes and dislikes. From the replies it seems that the same kind of work may be found popular with volunteers in some organizations, and unpopular in others, because the two groups regard it quite differently. For example, 'visiting and befriending' comes third among the popular tasks and second among the unpopular ones: it is liked by some volunteers because they see it as a specific job, with a clear purpose, visible results, and providing social contacts: and disliked by others who consider that it is lonely work, without a clear purpose, and with no visible results. The kinds of work most often mentioned by voluntary organizations as being popular were, in the order given, short-term practical tasks involving contact with clients, work with old people, visiting and befriending, work with children, club work, hospital work and transport. Unpopular tasks were practical jobs not involving contact with clients, visiting and befriending, mental health work, work with adolescents, and visiting the deaf, blind, or others with special needs. The kinds of work referred to in these replies were not defined precisely and there is obviously some overlapping; for example, between 'work with old people' and 'visiting and befriending'. What is particularly interesting is not so much the kinds of work mentioned as the reasons given for their popularity or unpopularity, which were almost identical for all the popular tasks and for all the unpopular ones.

112   From these replies a fairly clear picture emerges of the factors which, in the opinion of voluntary organizations, cause volunteers to like or dislike particular kinds of work. Voluntary workers are thought to like jobs which have a clear purpose, results which can be seen, with a limited commitment, and which

are appreciated by their clients. Some of them find social contacts important, and do not like jobs in which they are working alone. In a number of different services there is a dislike of having to deal with 'difficult clients'. Some like tasks which they regard as simple; some dislike those which lack variety; and there is a sharp distinction between the practical manual jobs without contact with clients, which are regarded as 'chores', and those in which practical help is given directly to people who can be seen to benefit and who show appreciation. The fact that many volunteers seem to shrink from undertaking a long-term commitment needs considering. It is possible that some people take up voluntary work rather than paid employment just for this reason—because they cannot see the way clear to committing themselves to regular hours of work for an indefinite period. There may well be a genuine difficulty, and it would be foolish to lose good volunteers by insisting too strongly on the desirability of continuity. On the other hand, there may be some who hesitate simply because they do not know enough initially to be sure that they would want or would be able to continue for more than a short time. The other reasons given for jobs which are popular or unpopular all underline heavily the need for careful selection and allocation, for more thought about the right and wrong uses of voluntary help, for appropriate preparation of each volunteer for the work which he is undertaking to do, and, perhaps most important of all, for helpful support, guidance and encouragement while he is doing it.

Variations in the Distribution of Volunteers

113   We have attempted to indicate in fairly broad outline the kinds of work undertaken by volunteers at the present time. Clearly there is an enormous range of work to be done, and we are impressed by what we have learned of the continuing growth of voluntary service and the way in which it is branching out in many directions. Goodwill and readiness to volunteer can be seen on all sides: we believe that there is practically no section of society from which volunteers could not be found, and we are convinced that there are still many untapped resources to be drawn upon. In almost every field of work affecting the welfare

of people there is a place for voluntary help, and in many services the needs are so varied that people of widely different types and abilities can make a contribution. At present, however, the use of voluntary help is very uneven. One reason for this may be the special difficulty of providing some types of service in rural areas. Citizens' Advice Bureaux are experimenting with mobile bureaux and with other ways of reaching rural users, but for visiting services the problems are not easy to overcome. The great advantage of voluntary workers possessing their own transport tends to limit the field of recruitment; and often the right volunteer for a particular client may live too far away for frequent visiting. There is also difficulty about using local volunteers in work of a personal and confidential kind in rural communities where people do not wish those living near them to discuss their personal affairs. Services in rural areas will inevitably have to face these difficulties, but with the increasing mobility of the population generally they may become less acute.

114   Information which we have received both in reply to the questionnaire sent to voluntary organizations and from other sources indicates that by far the largest numbers of volunteers at present are engaged either in work for the elderly or in the youth service. Many of them are attached to the large organizations which operate all over the country, but even in these organizations the distribution is patchy. For example, the National Old People's Welfare Council told us that while the average number of voluntary visitors in the eighteen local old people's welfare organizations from which they obtained information for us was 168, one of these, in an urban district, had only four, and another, in a county borough, had 765. Discrepancies such as this cannot be entirely due to differences in population and in social need.

115   It is clear that certain services can use considerably larger numbers of volunteers than others: the numbers required must be affected by the kind of work for which they are needed and the way in which it is organized. Some of the agencies which use fewer voluntary workers are those in which volunteers are undertaking skilled personal work such as is

described in paragraph 101. Great importance is attached to their selection and to preparation, training and consultation. Usually there is a professional staff, with whose work the volunteers are associated, and who are concerned with their training and guidance. In services of this kind the number of volunteers may be relatively small, but their work is often of a very high quality.

116   There remain some fields in which very little use is made of voluntary workers, although it seems likely that many more volunteers could make a valuable contribution in these services, and indeed there is fairly general agreement that this is so. We refer particularly to some voluntary organizations, such as the Invalid Children's Aid Association and Family Service Units; and to local authority children's departments and their mental health, welfare and education services. The pattern of development over the past twenty years seems to have been that the growth of voluntary work has been slowest in services where the place of social workers has been clearly recognized; and which have therefore needed both to emphasize the fact that much of their work calls for professional skill, and to concentrate on training and recruiting the qualified staff required. This has been the position of some of the voluntary bodies providing casework services, and also of the local authority social service departments. Local authorities have the additional problem of adapting their organization to include volunteers (and not all of them are flexible enough to do this readily) at a time when their resources are stretched to the utmost by the rapid expansion of their services and constant additions to their duties. There are signs, however, that this trend may now be reversed; and that many social workers now realize that a greater use of volunteers might enable them to help their clients more effectively.

117   If the main recommendations of the Seebohm Committee are put into effect, local authorities will be made responsible for providing not only an integrated social work service, but also a much more comprehensive one than exists at present. The Seebohm Report draws attention to gaps which need to be filled and weak places which need to be strengthened, but also

points out the inadequacy of the resources at present available to local authorities for this purpose. A combined local authority social service department, such as the Seebohm Committee has recommended, would provide scope for the increased use of voluntary help at many levels, both in services which are already the responsibility of the various local authority departments, and in new or extended services. It would also make it easier to rationalize procedures for dealing with volunteers. We should like to emphasize our complete agreement with the following extract from the Seebohm Report (para. 498):

'With the continuing growth of the personal social services it will be more and more necessary for local authorities to enlist the help of large numbers of volunteers to complement the teams of professional workers. . . . We have little doubt that there is a large untapped supply of such people who would willingly offer their services if the jobs were worthwhile, were clearly defined and shown to be relevant to present-day needs.'

The Proper Function of the Volunteer

118   We shall discuss the organization of voluntary work, and questions of recruitment, selection, preparation and training later in this report, but it may be as well, at this point, to look at what we believe to be another reason for unevenness in the use of voluntary workers, namely the lack of any clear policy or agreement as to what their proper function is and in what ways the services which they offer can most appropriately be used. We have already seen something of the diversity of opinions held by administrators of services using voluntary workers, by social workers, and by volunteers themselves. The view of the great majority, and one with which we entirely agree, is that volunteers should not be regarded as substitutes for professional workers. The suggestion, made by many of our witnesses, that volunteers can save the time of qualified staff by relieving them of duties which do not require professional skill or knowledge, is one which needs careful examination, and which, if taken at its face value, might lead to misunderstanding. We certainly believe that the use of volunteers can lead to a better service; but

this cannot be achieved by employing fewer qualified staff. Social workers, in co-operation with volunteers, may be able to provide a fuller service, possibly to a greater number of clients: nurses can give better nursing care to their patients if voluntary workers can attend to some of the patients' other needs: trained youth leaders or community workers can, in similar ways, use the help of volunteers to make the service which they are offering a better one. Because professional staff who are helped by volunteers can concentrate more on the work for which their special skills are required, their own contribution becomes more valuable. At the same time, these professional workers, or other qualified persons (such as organizers or supervisors of voluntary service) will have to give time and thought to the volunteers and their needs, and this additional responsibility must be recognized and allowed for. One of the associations of local authority chief officers considered that a major advantage of using voluntary workers was that 'numbers are limitless'. Even if this is true the numbers that can be used satisfactorily and helpfully must always be limited by the agency's resources for recruitment, selection, preparation, organization, guidance and consultation, some or all of which will be required in varying degrees for all kinds of voluntary work.

119   Some voluntary organizations suggested that one way of extending the use of volunteers would be by using them for practical and 'menial' tasks in hospitals in order to release professional staff. Clearly, trained professional staff should be used to do the work for which they are qualified and paid, but is it right that this should be achieved by asking voluntary workers to undertake domestic or manual tasks in a service which is publicly financed? This is quite different, in our view, from giving to infirm or inadequate people, in their own homes, practical help of a kind which they can clearly be seen to need, and might otherwise be quite unable to obtain: such service, as we have seen, is willingly and appropriately given by many volunteers. There are, too, many who show an extraordinary readiness to undertake practical or domestic tasks in hospitals or other residential establishments, feeling that if the patient or

clients benefits this is justification enough. Others, however, have hinted that they are less happy to be used in this way. Voluntary organizations suggested that volunteers were sometimes exploited by being used as cheap labour, or 'to do dirty work for professionals', or, if they were used purely for practical chores, without ever being brought face to face with the people they were helping. In general, volunteers are very willing to do any kind of work in a real emergency, due, for example, to unavoidable temporary shortage of staff, illness, or some other crisis, and we see no objection to this: in fact, temporary gap-filling of this kind may be a very suitable way of harnessing the goodwill of the community. We have not, however, been able to arrive at any clear principles that would enable us to argue convincingly one way or the other as to whether in more normal circumstances volunteers should be asked to undertake tasks of a purely domestic or manual kind in any public service. Nevertheless, we are firmly of the view that it is necessary for all users of volunteers to differentiate clearly between their tasks and those for which paid labour is hired, and not to ask volunteers, except in an emergency, to undertake work which, in the setting concerned, is normally done by paid workers.

120   We believe that a clear distinction between practical tasks undertaken by voluntary workers and those for which paid staff are employed is in the best interests of both volunteers and staff, and most likely to contribute to the overall efficiency of the service. The willingness of many volunteers to undertake domestic or manual tasks is likely to be diminished if they consider they are being used as cheap labour or as a substitute for effective manpower policies. On the other hand there might well be a tendency for paid employees to lose confidence in managements that have no clear policy for distinguishing between their work and tasks which are given to volunteers. Such a deterioration in morale, and the feelings of insecurity that may go with it, are likely to aggravate management's problem of maintaining an adequate manual labour force. But of even greater consequence is that the indiscriminate use of volunteers might well cover up serious deficiencies in the management of the service. A report from the National Board of

Prices and Incomes in March 1967, on a reference that included manual workers in the National Health Service, stated, for example, that there was plenty of room for improvement in the utilization of its manual labour force. In such a situation the use of volunteers to bridge gaps due to shortage of labour might only further delay the corrective measures that are required.

121   These considerations are not put forward as an argument for fixing once and for all the boundaries between tasks done by paid labour and by volunteers. Indeed, our aim is to enable the development of voluntary work to be properly planned in the light of changing circumstances affecting the provision of the social services, and the difficulties that those who provide the services are likely to face in the availability of manpower. It is quite possible that such changes will lead to a widening of the tasks for which volunteers are used. We consider, therefore, that users of voluntary help will need to keep constantly under review the tasks which are given to volunteers, in the light of the total needs of the service, and as part of the formulation of an overall manpower policy. Adequate consultation and negotiations with staff and unions must take place where changes are considered desirable in the distribution of work between paid staff and volunteers; and any arrangements made for the use of volunteers in manual and domestic tasks must be such that volunteers can see that their contribution is significant and is genuinely respected by the authorities and the paid staffs with whom they come into contact. We can sum this up by saying that if the tasks of volunteers are to be widened in these directions it will require all that is best in modern efficient management.

Ancillary Staff

122   Some mention should be made of the use of unqualified paid workers as ancillary staff in the child care, probation, and other services. This has some bearing on the question of how volunteers should be used, since, at first sight, there is a good deal of similarity between work suggested for these ancillary workers and that which is thought suitable for volunteers,

89

particularly in relieving qualified staff of work for which their qualifications are not specifically required. There is probably no clear distinction between functions appropriate to volunteers and to paid ancillary staff; but there are certain differences which lead us to the view that in some services there is likely to be a place for both. In the first place, most ancillary staff would presumably be working full time and would, therefore, be available to a greater degree and in a different way from volunteers. They would be subject to normal staff conditions and discipline, and they could be used in a variety of ways, sometimes on rather routine or humdrum jobs. They also form an additional source of help to the social services, by providing an opening for people who possess the qualities needed in a good volunteer or a future social worker but need full-time paid employment.

The Special Contribution of Voluntary Workers

123   The special gift which all volunteers offer, in many different ways, is their time; providing service to other people to an extent which could never be achieved solely by the employment of paid staff. Because they are giving their time and are, therefore, free from the feeling that their output of work must justify the salary they are paid, their relationships with their clients are often more relaxed and informal than those of paid workers: they can devote a great deal of time to one particular client or to a single piece of work if this seems desirable: and they are able to continue a relationship almost indefinitely without having to consider the possibly greater need of some new client whom there is a statutory obligation to help. Volunteers who are permanent residents in a locality are often able to provide greater continuity in relationships with clients than social workers, who have a scarcity value which encourages mobility. Most volunteers have the advantage that, as part-time workers with many other interests, they are less affected than full-time staff by the pressures and strains of the service in which they are working (an advantage which they share with many part-time paid staff); they can bring in something 'from outside' not only to their clients, but also to their full-time

colleagues in the work. They are also able to bring an independent judgment to bear on what they see of any service, and are thus in a position to offer constructive criticism as well as willingness to help. These are some of the attributes of voluntary workers which should be most highly prized, and made use of as fully as possible in the social services.

124   Voluntary workers who undertake arduous and regular duties for no reward need assurance that they have a positive and significant contribution to make. As we suggested earlier, lack of such assurance has no doubt contributed to the critical attitude which many volunteers display towards social workers and other paid staff. Equally, social workers need to consider and to appreciate the part which voluntary workers can play, and how they can best be used. In our view the most fruitful use of volunteers in the social services is as an extension of and complement to the work of qualified staff. They can often provide the practical help which may be an important element in any personal service. They can offer an unhurried befriending and supporting relationship, and are helped in this if there is a short-term goal which gives purpose to their work, and is a stage towards the social worker's long-term objective. Unless they are highly trained and professionally supported, they should not be expected to deal on their own with complex personal and family problems, difficulties arising as a result of mental disturbance, or matters involving delicate and confidential interpersonal relationships. In some circumstances the relationship between a volunteer and a client can develop into friendship, in a way which would be inappropriate in a professional relationship. There can also be a friendly relationship, though of a different and probably more temporary kind, between different generations, as when old people are visited by young volunteers, whom they may regard rather as they would grandchildren. There are clearly good grounds for believing that volunteers, just because their work is done voluntarily, can offer service which is of value to their clients, of a kind which could not be provided solely by the use of paid staff. There are also some people who hold the view that as the needs of the social services are almost unlimited, and resources are not, it is quite legitimate to regard voluntary work

as a way of extending services beyond the limits which considerations of economy might impose. We see nothing wrong with this view, provided that voluntary resources are not abused.

125   We are left with a conviction that the social services as we know them, and as they are developing, give almost unlimited scope for voluntary effort. The range of tasks available for volunteers is such that gifts and interests of every kind can be utilized. We believe that a careful examination of each service or area of need, preferably by a combination of the voluntary, professional and administrative interests involved in it, would prove very rewarding. It would be likely to lead to a reassessment of tasks and roles, and to greater clarity about immediate and long-term aims and the action needed to accomplish these.

Chapter 6

ORGANIZATION OF THE WORK OF VOLUNTEERS

The Purpose of Organization

126   It is very necessary in any service using volunteers that there should be some form of organization of their work. By organization we mean the provision of a system within and through which volunteers are enabled to carry out their work, as far as may be possible, effectively, smoothly and with satisfaction to their clients, themselves and the services which need their help. Unfortunately the word conveys to many people an impression of regimentation or of pushing people around, which is very far from what we have in mind. For this reason, we would have preferred to avoid the use of the term, and to find some designation other than 'organizer' for the responsible person; but we have not been able to find any convenient way of doing this and have, therefore, accepted the use of the word as inevitable.

127   Not all volunteers feel a need for organization: in fact there are some people who, however they understand the term, have a real horror of being organized; and some who, having been introduced to the work which they are going to do, can continue usefully and contentedly without being conscious of the system behind it. Pioneer movements often begin in a completely informal way, but an organizational structure will become necessary as the movement grows. At some stage, wherever voluntary help is being used, it will be necessary for some person or persons to undertake the work of 'organization' or 'management', of which the main functions are:

(a) to know where voluntary help is required, and to allocate volunteers to places where they are needed and to work which is suitable for them;

(b) to see that volunteers are used appropriately and safe-guarded from either exploitation or neglect;

(c) to ensure that volunteers are able to obtain the preparation or training which they need;

(d) to give support to volunteers in their work, and see that professional help is available for them as and when it is required;

(e) to ensure that any service for which volunteers are relied upon is provided to a proper standard, and that there are adequate arrangements for covering absences;

(f) to provide volunteers with opportunities for meeting one another for mutual encouragement and interest;

(g) to ensure that each volunteer understands the conditions of his work and the extent of his commitment, knows to whom he is accountable, and is informed about practical details such as entitlement to claim expenses, insurance schemes and so on.

The person carrying out this organizing function may also be responsible for other functions of at least equal importance, such as recruitment, selection, preparation or training, but this will not necessarily be so. Those responsible for the organization of voluntary work will, however, need to satisfy themselves that all these resources are available, to be fully informed about them, and to work very closely with those who are providing them.

Development of Organization by Statutory Bodies

128   Until recently, the organization of the work of volunteers was carried out almost exclusively by voluntary bodies. Councils of Social Service, Settlements, agencies providing a wide variety of services, and specialized bodies devoted to one particular kind of work, have recruited volunteers and organized their work in various ways. Some of these bodies initially depended solely on volunteers, but there are now very many which have a nucleus of paid staff who may be engaged in either administration or field work and who may, but often do not,

include qualified social workers. Many services which were previously run by voluntary bodies and staffed mainly by volunteers have now become the responsibility of local authorities; and in some cases the result of this was that the use of voluntary workers was abruptly terminated. More recently there has been a move towards the establishment of a partnership, the voluntary bodies continuing to recruit workers and to make them available to assist with the statutory services. There are a few outstanding examples of statutory services which for many years have directly recruited and organized voluntary workers, among them the Youth Service and the School Care Committees of the London County Council, now of the Inner London Education Authority: but these are the exceptions, and outside these services the vast majority of volunteers have been and still are attached to voluntary organizations. There are, however, clear and significant signs now that the recruitment and organization of volunteers directly by statutory services is gathering momentum: in some fields, particularly in hospitals and in the probation and after-care service, it is already being actively developed and officially encouraged.

129   We have already referred to the work of volunteers in hospitals, and to the survey carried out by King Edward's Hospital Fund for London of the work of organizers of voluntary services. The impetus to the appointments of organizers made during the past few years was given in a circular issued by the Ministry of Health in 1962, in which the whole emphasis was on enlisting and organizing as fully as possible the help which could be provided by voluntary bodies and the volunteers whom they could make available. It has been found, however, that the appointment of organizers has resulted in a great increase in the direct recruitment of volunteers: of a sample of voluntary workers in hospitals employing organizers, who were questioned in the course of the survey, only 31 per cent said that they had entered the work through membership of a voluntary organization.

130   In the field of probation and after-care, the recruitment of volunteers directly, as well as through voluntary organiza-

tions, is being actively encouraged by the Home Office. Following the publication in 1963 of the report 'The Organisation of After-Care' by the Advisory Council on the Treatment of Offenders, the Home Office issued a circular in November 1965, on the Use of Volunteers. In this circular Probation Committees were advised that the whole field of potential recruitment of volunteers should be surveyed, and that this would include recruitment directly by probation officers as well as through religious bodies and voluntary organizations. Responsibility for the selection and appointment of volunteers would, however, rest formally with local Probation Committees. More recently, the Working Party on the Place of Voluntary Service in After-Care, appointed by the Home Office under the Chairmanship of the Dowager Marchioness of Reading, in its Second Report published in 1967, distinguished between 'associates', that is volunteers 'who can provide support for a considerable period by a personal relationship'; and other volunteers 'whose contribution is more likely to be of short duration in the way of a simple practical task or advice on a technical problem not requiring close personal involvement'. The Working Party recommended that Probation Committees should recruit and accredit their own associates, but recognized that other volunteers might be recruited either directly or through voluntary organizations, and might operate within their own organizations or be used individually by probation officers. It also drew attention to the fact that 'there will always be truly independent persons and organisations who do not want any official contact or recognition and yet wish to offer a service to such offenders as care to make use of them'.

131   Although voluntary bodies have for many years given valuable help to local authorities, both in the provision and staffing of residential establishments and in the community care of old and handicapped persons, the direct recruitment and use of volunteers by local authorities themselves has been very limited and, until recently, largely confined to work in child welfare centres, some clinics, clubs, and homes of various kinds. Now a start has been made by certain authorities in recruiting voluntary workers directly and using them to complement the

work of their own field staff. Such arrangements are found at present mainly in Welfare Departments, but Children's Departments, too, are beginning to use volunteers in their work with families.

132   The Seebohm Committee clearly envisaged that this movement towards the direct use of voluntary help by local authorities would continue and would be an important element in the development of the social service departments, the establishment of which was the main recommendation of that Committee. In paragraph 498 of the Seebohm Report it is stated, 'the social service department must become a focal point to which those who wish to give voluntary help can offer their services', and in paragraph 499: 'The direct use of voluntary workers by local authority departments will involve a working out of functions which may only come about gradually after experiment. Meanwhile, there are advantages in working through existing organisations which would recruit the volunteers.' This might be taken to imply that in the opinion of the Seebohm Committee the role of voluntary bodies as providers and users of voluntary work in the social services is a diminishing or even a dying one: but, as we have stated in Chapter 1, this is not our view. There are many references in that Committee's Report to the continuing work of voluntary bodies, for example (paragraph 496): 'The social service department should play an important part in giving support, both financial and professional, to vigorous outward looking voluntary organisations which can demonstrate good standards of service, provide opportunities for appropriate training for their workers, both professional and voluntary, and show a flair for innovation.'

Present Patterns of Organization

133   There are at the present time, and we believe that there must continue to be, a number of different ways in which the help of voluntary workers is obtained, organized and used. Volunteers may work:

(a) as members of a voluntary body undertaking a particular type of work, responsible for its own policy and for the provision of a service, with or without support from public funds: examples of such bodies are Marriage Guidance Councils, Samaritans, Citizens' Advice Bureaux;

(b) in a service or scheme provided by a voluntary organiza-tion in association with a local authority or other public body which provides financial support and may exercise control over policy: for example in youth clubs, some children's holiday schemes, provision of meals on wheels;

(c) as members of an organization recruiting volunteers for work of a variety of different kinds within public services such as hospitals, old people's welfare and other local authority services: such volunteers are responsible in their work to the service which uses their help, but remain members of their voluntary organization: for example the Women's Royal Voluntary Service, British Red Cross Society, Community Service Volunteers;

(d) as volunteers directly recruited by and attached to a hospital, school, local authority department or other public body;

(e) in a service provided and staffed by a public body, but operating from premises unconnected with that body and working as a separate entity: this is a newly developing pattern of which one of the few examples at present is the Blackfriars Family Counsellors Project, provided by a local authority (the London Borough of Southwark) and operating as an activity of the Blackfriars Settlement.

The classification given above, like others in this report, is not clear-cut. The categories overlap to some extent, and the work of some organizations can be included in more than one category.

134   With these varying patterns it is neither desirable nor possible to envisage any standard system of organization. Voluntary bodies have their own arrangements for organizing the work of volunteers, with varying degrees of effectiveness. Some of these bodies appear to have given little thought to aspects of organization which go beyond the acceptance and allocation of volunteers: while in some quarters there seems to be an idea that organization will be resented by volunteers,

that it implies a kind of discipline which ought not to be imposed upon voluntary workers, or that it would detract from the spontaneity of their work and their 'unofficial' approach. These fears seem to be unfounded, since many volunteers themselves have made it clear that they welcome the kind of help and encouragement which a proper scheme of organization can provide. Comments by volunteers, a number of which have already been quoted or referred to, point to the need in many services, both statutory and voluntary, for better arrangements for allocation of jobs, briefing and information, and more definite links between volunteers and the organizations to which they are attached. This need is felt in varying degrees by voluntary workers of many kinds and of all ages. For example, members of one organization primarily for young people were critical of the lack of communication with their headquarters, and felt that their organization showed no interest in them as people or in their progress in the work which they had been sent to do. They also referred to the fact that when sent off to jobs they had felt quite inadequately informed of what would be expected of them. In another service a group of workers from different clubs of the same kind much appreciated the fact that the meeting arranged for them with members of this Committee enabled them also to meet one another. They said that they had never before had an opportunity of discussing what they were doing with other people doing similar work. The need also shows itself in the feeling among volunteers that some are called upon too frequently, or that too much is asked of them; while others are under-used, or are given work which does not enable them to make their fullest contribution. The common need of all these people is for some person, or persons, with a direct concern for individual volunteers, their suitability for the work which they are doing, their progress in it, and its effectiveness in relation to their clients and to the service; in fact the organizer of voluntary work.

Examples of Organization of Voluntary Work in Public Services

135   The organizers of voluntary services in hospitals, although so far only a small minority of hospitals employ them,

and their work is still at a comparatively early stage, provide one example of the role and functions of an organizer. In the first instance, unless the person appointed is very familiar with the setting, he or she needs to spend considerable time in getting to know the staff, enlisting their interest and co-operation, and becoming familiar with the way the service works, and its methods. This is particularly important in an establishment such as a hospital, which has its own traditions, and is staffed by members of different professions and occupations, not all of whom are likely to be fully persuaded of the value of voluntary service. The report by King Edward's Hospital Fund mentions that this process could take anything from one to six months, and goes on to describe the various components of the organizer's job. They include inevitably a certain amount of administrative and office work, but generally speaking personal contacts with volunteers and with staff are regarded as much the most important part of the work. Naturally, the emphasis is not the same everywhere, but in general the main elements in the work of organizers in hospitals appear to be: keeping in touch with all departments and their staff in order to learn about their requirements and to discuss existing and new ways of using voluntary help; direct recruiting efforts and the interviewing of prospective new volunteers; fitting volunteers to work appropriate to their wishes and abilities and introducing them to the staff with whom they are to work; arranging rotas or teams of volunteers when necessary, to ensure that work for which they are relied upon is always covered; maintaining contact, as far as possible, with all volunteers, knowing how they are progressing, and being available for individual discussion with any one who needs explanation or encouragement; arranging meetings for volunteers, either as social occasions or to provide opportunities for briefing and discussion. Other important aspects of the work of these organizers are attendance at staff meetings, giving talks to groups of staff, maintaining liaison with other voluntary groups in the hospital, and speaking at meetings of groups and organizations outside.

136   Another example, in a different kind of service, and on a very different scale, is given in evidence from the Association

of Child Care Officers. They quote a county borough in which the Children's Department has a register of voluntary workers, recruited directly by the department. These volunteers undertake befriending and supportive visiting of families in difficulties, and a social worker on the staff, assisted by a voluntary secretary is responsible for organizing their work. The organizer undertakes the initial interview and selection, followed by a preliminary discussion, after which the volunteer is put in touch with a particular family and subsequently works in close co-operation with the child care officer concerned with the family. Work with the family is discussed with the child care officer, but in addition there are regular meetings of the whole group of volunteers, with the organizer, for the purpose of general discussion, criticism and teaching. This is a small scheme with, at the time when it was described, thirteen voluntary workers, of whom eight were either professionally qualified social workers or had a social science qualification. This example is in several respects exceptional, but there is good reason to suppose that similar schemes could be undertaken in other places and with less qualified volunteers.

137   The former London County Council, a pioneer among local authorities both in the employment of social workers and in the large scale use of voluntary workers, built up a School Care Committee service which was of outstanding interest and importance in the pre-war years. The basis of this service, established in 1909, was that school care committees, composed entirely of voluntary workers, were made responsible for ensuring, as far as possible, that no child was prevented by lack of food, clothing, or medical attention from taking full advantage of the education provided. A staff of paid workers, known as organizers, was appointed to recruit and guide the volunteers, but to take little or no part in the visiting of homes and other personal work on behalf of children and their families. This work, which has been extended to include visiting the homes of children presenting problems of behaviour and other social problems, is carried out almost exclusively by the voluntary workers. The organizers are still for the most part people with basic qualifications in social science but without professional training; and

there have until very recently been no systematic arrangements for the training of voluntary workers. The organizers, now in the ratio of about one to twenty volunteers, remain in the background, advising volunteers and complementing their work; but rarely undertaking direct personal work. We are aware that the Social Research Unit of Bedford College, in 1965–66, carried out an enquiry into the School Care Committee service as part of a research project covering the social welfare services of the Inner London Education Authority. Their findings have not been published, but we understand that following this enquiry some reorganization of the service is being considered. We believe that the need for some reappraisal of the respective functions of voluntary workers and organizers is recognized, and that the volunteers would welcome more help and guidance from professionally qualified staff in their dealings with families in difficulty.

138   Local authorities are showing increasing interest in the idea of using voluntary workers directly. The opinion given in the evidence received in 1967 from one of the associations of local authority officers that 'it is only through well organized bodies (i.e. voluntary bodies) that local authorities can make effective use of voluntary help' is, we believe, no longer representative. In some authorities, including a number of London boroughs, voluntary service liaison officers (sometimes called community service officers) have been appointed in the welfare departments. The primary purpose of these appointments seems to have been to provide liaison with the many voluntary bodies whose volunteers were assisting the authorities, and to coordinate their work. Some of the liaison officers appear to confine their activities to this work, but others are now also engaged in the direct recruitment of volunteers and in introducing them to appropriate tasks. We can see that there is a useful role for these officers, but doubt whether it has been sufficiently worked out or exploited.

139   The Probation and After-Care service, coming relatively late to using volunteers, has developed several different patterns of organization. In some parts of the country, volun-

teers are recruited direct by the probation officers with whom they work. In other areas an officer, often of senior rank, takes the responsibility as part of his total work. In Inner London a voluntary body, Teamwork Associates, was established in 1966 to recruit, prepare and supervise volunteers on behalf of the service. This, and other voluntary bodies already operating in the area, were accredited by the Probation and After-Care Committee to work as its agents in this field. The Prisoners' Wives service, an organization specializing in the care of families of men serving custodial sentences, was similarly accredited. The distinctive feature of both Teamwork Associates and the Prisoners' Wives service has been their close working relationship with officers of the statutory service, both at management and field level. At the end of 1968 nearly 200 volunteers in the Inner London area were in regular contact with clients. Each volunteer was a member of a group meeting at frequent intervals with its consultant probation officer. In those cases where the client was subject to statutory licence, the probation officer necessarily continued to carry the official responsibility.

Volunteer Bureaux and Clearing Houses

140   An important contribution to the organization of voluntary work is now being made by Councils of Social Service. Twenty-three of these Councils have established volunteer bureaux, of which eight, financed by local authority grants and by Trusts, have full-time or part-time paid organizers: one bureau is financed by a national Trust and three, in London, by grants from a regional Trust. Eight bureaux are organized by staff of the Councils of Social Service, and seven are run by voluntary organizers. Twelve bureaux provide a service specifically for young people, and in addition twenty-three Councils of Social Service act as clearing houses for community service by young people. Clearing houses for young people have also been set up by Task Force in a number of London boroughs, and in a few places outside London by the Young Volunteer Force Foundation or by other bodies.

141   The main function of volunteer bureaux is to collect information about the needs and opportunities for voluntary

service in their areas, to provide a centre to which volunteers may come for advice and information, and to refer them to appropriate organizations in which their help can be used. One of the most active of these bureaux is that provided by the Camden Council of Social Service. At this bureau, in the year February 1967–January 1968, 422 volunteers were interviewed, and 320 of these were referred to other organizations: others found opportunities for voluntary work in some of the activities of the Camden Council of Social Service itself. The fifty-one other organizations to which these volunteers were referred included departments of the Camden Borough Council, a number of local voluntary bodies, some national voluntary organizations, and about twelve hospitals. Some bureaux also advise volunteers about suitable educational courses, and some arrange discussion groups or seminars for volunteers.

142   Some of the young people's clearing houses are more than bureaux, and take on in addition some characteristics of the organizations described briefly in paragraph 133(c) above. Like the bureaux, they collect information about needs, endeavour to stimulate greater awareness of the potential contribution of voluntary help, and introduce individuals or groups of volunteers to services which need them; and these are their main functions. In some, however, particularly those set up by Task Force and the Young Volunteer Force Foundation, the staff, for the most part themselves young people, accept responsibility for maintaining contact with their members, and for exercising a degree of supervision over their work. They also make it their business to discover needs which are not being met by any existing organization and to find and organize volunteers to meet these needs.

143   It is interesting to note that in none of the London boroughs in which voluntary service liaison officers have been appointed was there at the time of the appointment a Council of Social Service. Where Councils of Social Service exist, and establish some form of bureau for volunteers, they are able to meet a need of which both local authorities and voluntary bodies using volunteers must be conscious. Such an arrangement in no

way takes the place of the organization of voluntary work which is required within any particular service: but it is easy to see the advantages of having in any area a central source from which all would-be volunteers can obtain advice and comprehensive information, and can be referred to agencies needing the kind of help which they are able to give. It helps volunteers by providing one point of enquiry instead of many: it also relieves individual social service agencies of the need to provide their own arrangements for giving preliminary information and passing on to other agencies any volunteers whom they are unable to accept, but who may be willing and able to undertake other work. An essential condition is that there should be full confidence and co-operation between the bureau and the organizations which require voluntary help. Our evidence shows that, as far as existing bureaux are concerned, there is generally no difficulty about this; though the organizer of one bureau comments that there was at first some misunderstanding and suspicion, and that a good deal of work was needed to explain to local organizations that the purpose of the bureau was to find volunteers for them and not to take them away. After that relations were described as good. In areas where there is no Council of Social Service or other voluntary body willing and with the necessary resources to provide a service of this kind, it might possibly be provided by the local authority, operating on behalf of its own services and also of all other statutory and voluntary bodies needing volunteers. There are, however, advantages in such a service being provided by some body which is not itself a major user of voluntary help, and can, therefore, be regarded as neutral. A better arrangement, therefore, in places where there are no existing facilities, might be the establishment of an independent bureau, set up by joint statutory and voluntary initiative, and with financial support from the statutory bodies.

144   In whatever way this advisory and information service for volunteers is provided we should not wish to suggest that all offers of help should necessarily go through it, or that volunteers should be discouraged from making a direct approach to any statutory or voluntary body if they prefer to do so. Some people may be specially attracted to a particular organization or

type of work about which they know enough to be sure that this is what they want to do. Organizations using voluntary help should, therefore, be prepared to receive such direct offers of help, and to refer to the bureau any volunteer whose services they are unable to use and who is willing to be considered for some other work.

The Organizer of Voluntary Work

145   The sort of person needed to organize voluntary work in any service, and the type of organizational structure will depend on a number of factors; particularly, of course, on the kind of service provided and the ways in which volunteers are to be used. Personal interest in and concern for the volunteers themselves will always be necessary; but, while in some services familiarity with the work which volunteers will be doing and the demands which it will make on them is of prime importance, there are others in which the need is much more for general organizing ability. Social workers, in their evidence to us, thinking of services in which volunteers would be associated with them in work involving close personal relationships with clients, seemed to take it for granted that the organizer of voluntary services should himself be a social worker. This view was echoed by the Home Office in their evidence relating to voluntary work in the field of child care, where they said, 'there is much force in the view that voluntary help, if it is to be successfully used in any social service, requires a professional member of staff with special responsibility for organisation and training'. We would not disagree with this view in relation to work in which volunteers are working closely with social workers, where the number of volunteers is relatively small in relation to the social work staff, and where training is so essential that it is difficult to separate it from organization. The really important factor, particularly at this stage in the development of the use of volunteers, is that the organizer should be sensitive to, and able to share, the problems of social workers as well as those of the volunteers.

146   Where volunteers are visiting and befriending people who are lonely, isolated or housebound, the organizer must be

familiar with the various ways in which additional help can be obtained if the voluntary visitor comes to know of special difficulties which are beyond his scope: but the organizer need not necessarily be a professional. In work of this kind, continuity is important, and clients are likely to prefer to be visited by someone whom they know. One task of the organizer might be, therefore, the planning of small teams of volunteers, so that, if at any time a regular visitor is not available, his place can be taken by one of not more than two or three others who are already, or will become, known to the client. Where large numbers of volunteers are engaged in work of a more practical and less personal kind, it is vitally important to ensure that there are always enough of them for any particular piece of work. In information services one of the main functions of an organizer is to see that the workers are kept supplied with all the necessary information. People with the ability required for organizing these kinds of voluntary work are already to be found among volunteers themselves, and there is no reason why volunteers should not be used much more widely in the work of organization, not only by voluntary bodies but also in the statutory services. We hope that greater attention will be paid to the recruitment of people with appropriate ability and experience for this work, and to the preparation or training which they will need.

Relations With Voluntary Organizations

147   One problem which may face the organizer of voluntary work in a service which uses volunteers who are members of other organizations, particularly the large uniformed bodies, is the relationship of the volunteer to the parent organization on the one hand and to the service in which he is working on the other. Members of the uniformed organizations usually have strong feelings of loyalty towards these bodies and pride in their membership, and it is right that this should be so. But once a volunteer has undertaken work in any service his accountability to that service for the work which he is doing must take priority. Provided that the voluntary bodies concerned accept and encourage this, there is no reason why there should be any

conflict. Difficulties have, however, been known, and some are referred to in the report on Organizers of Voluntary Services in Hospitals. Some large voluntary bodies regard the provision of emergency services as their main responsibility, and consider that they should retain the right to recall their members from other work in the event of any disaster or emergency. Some wish their members to remain accountable to them and to consider themselves first and foremost as members of the particular organization, wherever they may be working. The wearing of uniform may also lead to difficulties; for example, if volunteers working in a hospital are expected to wear the uniform of their organization, while the hospital prefers all its voluntary workers to wear a particular type of overall. Such difficulties, if they persist, are likely to hamper the smooth running of the work of volunteers, and it is important, therefore, to distinguish between the volunteer's allegiance to the organization which enrolled him, and his accountability, while at work, to the service in which he is engaged.

148   There are two issues here: one of them, the question of volunteers being available to their parent organization if required for emergency work, is comparatively straightforward. If a voluntary organization undertakes to provide help in emergencies, such as floods, serious accidents, or disasters which render numbers of people homeless, and enrols people who are willing to be used in this way, it is perfectly legitimate that it should expect to be able to call on them when required. Such people know that, like lifeboat crews or retained firemen, they must give such emergency calls priority over whatever else they may have on hand. They may, however, also wish to undertake some other form of voluntary work regularly, and it should be possible for the service which uses their help to arrange this in such a way that if one, or even a group of them, is called off unexpectedly for emergency work no serious difficulty or hardship is caused. Provided that there is mutual understanding and co-operation between the agencies concerned, and good organization, there should be no real problem; though this situation will, no doubt, affect the kinds of work which can be given to these volunteers.

149   Apart from the fact that some volunteers may be called upon for emergency work there is always a need for the organizer in any service which receives volunteers from other bodies to recognize and respect the loyalty of these volunteers to the body of which they are members. There is no doubt that some voluntary workers find in their membership of a large organization, a sense of identity and companionship which may be lacking in the service in which they are working. We have seen in Chapter 3 that there are many people for whom the motive of making and enjoying human contacts is a potent one, outweighing their interest in any particular type of work. Such people, rather than attaching themselves directly to a particular service, may prefer to join a large organization which, as well as offering a variety of different kinds of work, provides companionship and a sense of corporate membership.

150   This type of arrangment is less appropriate for volunteers who will undertake work of a more personal kind, which calls for a greater degree of involvement and requires more in the way of preparation, training and continuing guidance. There is, as we have seen, a tendency towards an increasing use of volunteers in work involving close personal relationships; and with it a move towards the direct recruitment and guidance of volunteers by the agencies providing the services. This is natural, since agencies which are using voluntary workers for skilled and responsible tasks will want to have the first call on their services, to arrange for their training and guidance, and to know that there is no conflict of loyalties or of direction. The trend towards direct recruitment and training of volunteers is seen both in voluntary organizations, such as the Samaritans and some of the new movements, for example, the Simon Community, and in statutory bodies; and it appears likely that it will continue. The development of volunteer bureaux, from which prospective volunteers could obtain information and advice about opportunities for service, might result in still more direct recruitment by specialized agencies of people who, without the help of a bureau, would not have known what kind of work they wanted to do. In some services which need volunteers for a variety of tasks, the two methods of enrolment may, however, continue

side by side, as is happening at present in hospitals and in some local authority departments.

151   Statutory and voluntary bodies which recruit, train and use volunteers in services for which they are responsible should give careful consideration to the volunteers' need for a sense of identity and companionship, such as can be given by membership of a corporate body. Good organization and management can eliminate much of the feeling of isolation and lack of support which too many volunteers seem to experience at present; but some volunteers, particularly in services where their number is small and they are working individually, may need more than this. They may require something which will take the place of the professional associations of social workers and other staff; which will enable them to meet voluntary workers from other services, both for social activities and for discussion of their work; and which may be a means through which they can have a voice in the development of policy. Any movement of this kind would probably, in the first instance, be a local one, brought into being by volunteers themselves; but the staff of organizations which use voluntary workers can aid these developments by stimulating discussion, and, where appropriate, offering encouragement or advice.

Expenses and Insurance

152   A question related to organization, to which we have given our attention, is that of the repayment to voluntary workers of expenses incurred by them in carrying out their work. We have enquired about the present practices and views of statutory and voluntary bodies using voluntary help, and have also sought the views of volunteers themselves. We have been surprised at the wide variations both in practice and in attitudes to this question. There seems to be general agreement among officers of local authorities that the out-of-pocket expenses of voluntary workers should be paid: it appears that this is the normal practice in children's departments, but that it is less general in other departments of the local authorities. In evidence regarding the use of volunteers in local authority health ser-

vices, we were told that: 'Reimbursement of travelling and out-of-pocket expenses appears to be only fairly common'; and in welfare departments that: 'there is a lingering reluctance to meet travelling and out-of-pocket expenses but this is now being faced up to by the more progressive authorities'. There seems to be a feeling in some quarters that arrangements for payment of expenses might be abused and that caution is needed. 'The dividing line between payment of travelling and out-of-pocket expenses and payment for service is very fine, and great care must be exercised to ensure that reimbursement is made only of expenses which have actually been incurred.' Some local authority officers believe that it is easier for a volunteer to obtain payment of his expenses if he is a member of a voluntary body receiving a grant from the authority than if he is working for the authority direct.

153   Despite the belief that some voluntary organizations may be more ready to repay expenses than local authorities are, a substantial minority of the voluntary bodies which gave us information about their practices said that they did not pay expenses: and of those which were prepared to do so, only a minority said that they were usually claimed. The expenses for which repayment was offered included travelling, postal and telephone expenses, occasionally secretarial expenses, and in one case domestic help. Young volunteers, for example, members of International Voluntary Service, and Community Service Volunteers, may receive pocket money, usually of about thirty shillings weekly, particularly when engaged on long projects.

154   Voluntary workers themselves also expressed varying opinions. Of the 114 volunteers interviewed in the study carried out by the Institute of Community Studies, only eleven received anything in the way of expenses, though thirty considered that expenses ought to be paid; forty-seven thought that they ought not to do be paid; and the remainder had no strong views. Four of those who considered that expenses ought not to be paid said that their organization could not afford to pay: others made such comments as: 'If you want payment you shouldn't take on the job'; and 'I think it's a bit mean to claim.' It seemed to the

interviewer that some organizations had not made it clear enough to their workers that out-of-pocket expenses could be paid, or had even given the impression that claims were discouraged. There was similar divergence among the views of the groups of volunteers who were interviewed by members of the the Committee. A group of young volunteers working on fairly long projects, and without any paid employment, found their pocket money of thirty shillings 'a challenge': some of them found it difficult to meet their personal expenses, and they thought that two pounds would have been reasonable.

155   In our opinion voluntary workers should not be required to meet the cost of travelling or other expenses necessarily incurred in the course of their work. In some circumstances it may be reasonable for organizations using voluntary help also to pay the travelling expenses of volunteers to and from the place where they are working. It should be accepted that expenses can be paid, and it should be made as easy as possible for those who wish to do so to claim and obtain them. It is wrong that there should be any feeling that volunteers are not expected to claim, that it is mean or grasping to do so, or that there should be any embarrassment for volunteers who cannot afford to incur expense.

156   The question of insurance of voluntary workers is another which must not be overlooked. Some organizations already operate schemes for insuring their volunteers, and it is a matter which should be considered by every body which uses voluntary help. Each volunteer should be given information, on starting work, about the arrangments which exist, and should understand clearly what safeguard he has in the event of injury or damage occurring in the course of his work. Volunteers who use their own cars should be reminded of the need to satisfy themselves that their insurance policies provide cover for the use of their cars in the ways required in their work.

Identification of Voluntary Workers

157   Another related question is that of providing volunteers with some means by which they can be identified as genuine

representatives of the service or agency for which they are working. There may well be occasions on which voluntary workers will find it helpful to be able to produce some evidence of their bona fides; and an even more important consideration is the protection of clients from imposters. A uniform can be regarded as a means of identification, and some organizations provide badges for their workers, which serve a similar purpose. Probably the most satisfactory arrangement is for each volunteer to have a card, giving his own name and that of the service or organization represented, and signed by a responsible person. This is particularly important for workers who are engaged in visiting people in their own homes. It may also be helpful for such volunteers to be provided with a supply of leaflets, which can be handed to clients, giving information, about the organization, and the address and times at which the volunteer can be reached, or a message left for him.

158   In the Probation and After-Care service the term 'accredited associates' is used for those volunteers who are specifically appointed by Probation Committees to 'provide support for a considerable period by a personal relationship'. They are thus differentiated from those volunteers whose contribution is more likely to be of short duration and not requiring close personal involvement. This system is seen as different from, and rather more than a means of, identification. It signifies that the volunteer concerned holds a formal letter of appointment for a specified period, and that the Probation Committee accepts responsibility for the work which he does. It does not, however, necessarily denote a particular standard of training or proficiency.

Conclusions

159   We are convinced that the role of the organizer is of crucial importance in all services which use voluntary help. Although there are wide differences in types of organization, and therefore in the work of organizers, certain elements are always present; and one of the most important is the concern for each volunteer which will enable him to give of his best. In some

services it is desirable that the organizer should be a social worker; in others the duties of organizer may be undertaken by a paid worker who is not professionally qualified, or by a volunteer. It is probable that short courses of training for people, either paid or voluntary, who are selected to act as organizers of voluntary work, would be found extremely helpful. The Council for Training in Social Work suggested this in their evidence to us: among the matters mentioned as suitable for inclusion in such courses were the selection of volunteers, and some teaching about management, staff relations, group behaviour, and ethical principles. We agree that prospective organizers, whatever their background, would be likely to benefit from short courses on these lines.

160   Many services, and particularly those of local authorities, could well give much more attention to the organization of voluntary work than they have done so far. Unless a service has some real plan for using voluntary help, and some person responsible for seeing that it is used to the best advantage, there will continue to be a risk of unnecessary wastage of volunteers, of avoidable dissatisfaction and frustration, and fears of increasing rather than reducing the pressure on paid staff. The result is likely to be failure to obtain real benefit from what should be a valuable asset.

Chapter 7

RECRUITMENT AND SELECTION

Present Recruiting Practice

161   Active recruiting efforts still play only a limited part in bringing in voluntary workers. As we saw in Chapter 3, a high proportion of the volunteers who were interviewed in the course of special studies undertaken for the Committee had come to the work through personal contact with someone already involved. Others (15 per cent of those interviewed in the Hospital Survey, and 9 per cent in the study carried out by the Institute of Community Studies) said that they had themselves taken the initiative in offering help; and only a small proportion had joined as a result of any kind of publicity. This seems to be the general pattern at present, except perhaps in the organizations primarily for young people, where publicity, either in the press, through broadcasting, or in schools and colleges, is more deliberately used. There appears to be greater general awareness of the opportunities for service by young people, both at home and abroad, and of the work which they are doing, than of the many openings for older volunteers from all sections of the community.

162   Information given by voluntary organizations in reply to the question 'How are your volunteers recruited?' confirmed that personal introductions form the major source of recruitment. All the bodies whose replies to our questionnaire were analysed (see Appendix II) said that they used this method, and about half said that 75 per cent or more of their voluntary workers were recruited in this way. Other methods included the giving of talks to groups or other organizations, appeals through churches and schools, posters, and the issue of leaflets for display

in libraries and other public places or distribution to people thought likely to be interested. Citizens' Advice Bureaux were exceptional in making considerable use of advertising, though in this service, too, a high proportion of workers, perhaps as many as 50 per cent, are recruited through personal contacts. Some organizations appeared to have doubts as to whether general publicity would produce the 'right type' of volunteer: one said it had found that 'the real volunteer' was not usually as acceptable as those who had initially been recommended and then invited to apply. Similar views and practices were found among some of the other users of voluntary help. The Second Report of the Working Party on the Place of Voluntary Service in After-Care states:

'Experience generally, including that of the probation service, appears to support the view that personal approaches to known individuals are more likely to produce suitable volunteers than appeals to meetings or articles in the press. Leaflets have undoubted advantages over newspaper articles in that they result in a greater degree of selectivity in the choice of person at whom a recruiting drive is directed'.

In the London School Care Committee service new recruits are most usually obtained through existing voluntary workers who introduce friends and acquaintances, and general publicity is little used. Organizers of voluntary service in hospitals have made more use of publicity, sometimes advertising in the national press, but more often using articles in local papers, parish magazines or news sheets, and posters in public places: they too found, however, that the most successful means of recruitment was by existing volunteers bringing in others.

163   In some places Councils of Social Service are making a contribution towards the recruitment of volunteers for all local services, not only through the bureaux mentioned in the previous chapter, but also by other means. The Camden Council of Social Service issues a monthly newsletter, which makes known particular jobs for which volunteers are needed. One such list included a variety of interesting jobs, briefly but

adequately described, including work for teachers able to speak Greek or Indian languages; for a journalist or reporter; for a treasurer of a voluntary body (with some knowledge of book-keeping and accounting); for a scoutmaster for physically handicapped boys; as well as other work for which special knowledge would not be required. In some areas booklets have been produced giving comprehensive information about organizations needing voluntary help and the kinds of help required. Such booklets have been issued covering London, the North-West (south-east Lancashire and east Cheshire) and a few other areas.

164   In 1964 a general Guide to Voluntary Service written by David Hobman, then Information Officer of the National Council of Social Service, now Director of the Social Work Advisory Service, was published by H.M. Stationery Office. Mr Hobman has also given us information about his experience since the establishment of the Social Work Advisory Service (a service for providing information and advice on training and careers in social work) which underlines the pressing need for local bureaux or recruiting and advisory centres for volunteers. The Social Work Advisory Service receives a number of en-quiries, both from people who definitely wish to undertake voluntary work (and who may or may not be clear about the kind of work they wish to do) and from some who, having been uncertain initially, decide after discussion that some kind of voluntary work, rather than paid employment, is what they want. If such a person wishes to work in an area where there is a well-organized and effective volunteer bureau, it is easy to refer him there for information and advice; but in most places there is at present no such organization. The Social Work Advisory Service cannot itself undertake this work for volunteers, nor could any central agency expect to acquire and keep up to date all the detailed information which would be necessary. It is essential that such a service for volunteers should be locally based, both for the convenience of the volunteers themselves, and in order that local information shall always be available. We are convinced that for lack of such centres many volunteers are discouraged or lost.

Widening the Field of Recruitment

165   The concentration on recruitment through personal contacts naturally tends to limit the field from which voluntary workers are obtained, and perhaps to perpetuate recruitment from certain sections of society to the exclusion of others. We heard many references to the desirability of widening the field of recruitment, but we have little evidence of any real effort to do this, or of thought about ways in which it might be done. Some people justify the emphasis on recruitment of voluntary workers with a professional background on the grounds that such people are likely to know how to express themselves, and therefore how to communicate with others; and that a good educational standard is necessary in order that volunteers may be able to acquire the knowledge, and profit from the preparation and training, which are needed for many kinds of voluntary work. For some work a certain standard of education is a necessity, but not all volunteers require it at the same level, and clearly education is not confined to the professional classes. The expansion of educational opportunities and the widespread influence of mass media, by increasing the number of those who are aware of social issues and moved by them, have enormously extended the field of potential recruits. Moreover, it must be recognized that verbal ability is not the same as understanding, and to be articulate is not necessarily to be sensitive; the two may go together and may not.

166   Others argue that more volunteers should be recruited from the working class, on the grounds that people who are in difficulties can more easily be helped by those who can share with them a common background of experience. This is another assumption that cannot be accepted wholesale. Imagination and understanding are required, and a common background may be a help to volunteers in exercising these, but it is not essential. In organizations of the self-help type people are brought together by a common need, and by a desire to help not only themselves but those whose difficulties they share, and this attitude may also find expression in some kinds of work which are not consciously self-help movements. In other types of work,

however, there may be situations in which differences rather than similarities of background will be an advantage. In general, relationships are very much more dependent upon the character and personality of the individuals than upon their social background.

167   It seems to us that it is attitude rather than social background which is important, and the main object of extending the field of recruitment is to obtain more volunteers with understanding, sensitivity and the will to help. We know that more are needed and that the range of work open to them is immense. What is required is that organizations needing voluntary workers should consider first what kinds of people they want, in terms of age, sex and educational standards (if these are relevant), availability and personal qualities; and then how and where such people may be found. We asked voluntary organizations whether they had any comments to make on the kinds of volunteers whom they sought for particular services. A number of different qualities were mentioned in their replies, reliability being the one which occurred most frequently: next came the possession of experience or training, followed by common sense, ability, interest and understanding. Several organizations, however, replied by saying that they sought people who were 'suitable', or had the 'right' personality or temperament, or who were able to work in a particular situation, for example with a group, as members of a team, or with individuals. It did not appear that they had defined their needs in any specific way: they may indeed have decided that it was unnecessary to do so, either because of a general shortage of volunteers, or because they felt that they could provide opportunities of voluntary service for people of all kinds. Certainly the answers to this question did not suggest that criteria had been formulated, or point to any particular section of society as being more likely than another to produce the volunteers who were wanted.

Effects of Social Changes

168   In looking for new ways of bringing in volunteers, and new directions in which they may be sought, it must be remem-

bered that the availability of different sections of the community is affected by social changes. Changes which have occurred over the last twenty or thirty years include the tendency towards earlier marriage and child-bearing, increased use of family planning, shortage of domestic workers, more part-time employment of married women, or their return to full-time work when children are growing up, shorter working hours in some occupations, earlier retirement, often resulting in earlier promotion to responsible and demanding work. In their effect on people's availability for voluntary work some of these changes cancel one another out; and some may operate differently in different parts of the country, for example according to whether there is or is not a shortage of labour. They do, however, provide some pointers: they suggest that, as indeed we have found, there is likely to be a shortage of both men and women volunteers between the ages of 20 and 40, and that the service given by young people below this age will usually be of fairly short duration; but that there may be more people in full-time employment (other than housewives) who could give some time to voluntary work in the evenings. They also suggest that more women over 40 may have time to spare and that there may be considerable resources among the over-60s of both sexes. The increasing mobility of the population generally should be a help towards recruitment, particularly if a more realistic and generous attitude is taken towards the payment of expenses, and the lingering idea that only those who can afford to pay their own expenses should undertake voluntary work is finally abandoned.

Recruitment of Older Volunteers

169   At present retired people and those approaching retiring age form a numerically small part of the body of voluntary workers. Although there is growing awareness of the importance of preparing for retirement, and of planning for a full and active life after ceasing full-time employment, it does not seem to us that the possibilities of voluntary work are being brought sufficiently to the notice of older employed people. Pre-retirement courses are now held in many centres of adult education, and any such course should provide good opportunities for the

discussion of different kinds of voluntary work. One existing method of interesting older people is that developed by certain large firms which encourage members of their staff to visit and keep in touch with retired colleagues. These schemes include people of all ages, but it is hoped that among the older ones will be some who will continue to undertake some form of voluntary work after they themselves have retired.

170   Older people may well be able to provide the element of experience, and a number of the special skills, which many organizations seek in voluntary workers, and of which almost all say that they cannot find enough. We are convinced that a great deal more might be done in most services to identify particular jobs which could be undertaken by volunteers with special aptitudes, and to publicize them. A person who has some particular interest or skill is far more likely to offer help if he sees a description of an immediate opening which would give scope for his ability and experience, than if he learns of a quite general need for volunteers. The growing emphasis on efficient organization of voluntary work is likely to produce new opportunities for volunteers with organizing ability, particularly those who have experience of staff management: work of this kind might be particularly attractive to men in the years immediately following retirement from full-time employment. Other kinds of work, too, can benefit from the general experience, as well as the special knowledge, of professional and business men and women and of those who have had experience in industry.

The Organization of Recruitment

171   Possibly one reason for the apparent reluctance of some bodies, both statutory and voluntary, to publicise widely their need for volunteers is their realization of the work which would inevitably be entailed, both in the publicity itself and in sorting out the offers of help received as a result. It is quite often found in any recruiting activity that only a minority of the resulting offers can be used. Unless there is some person with definite responsibility for volunteers and some system for recruitment and allocation, it is quite likely that no-one will feel able to give

the necessary time, and the idea may well be abandoned on the grounds that the number of useful volunteers obtained is likely to be too small to make the effort worth while.

172   Whatever the work for which volunteers are sought, and whatever recruiting methods are adopted, it is important not to undervalue the work or the demands which it will make on the workers. Asking too little of people is a common mistake, due perhaps to a fear of frightening away potential volunteers before they have had a chance to become interested; or to an assumption that too much ought not to be asked of people who are giving their time and services voluntarily. To undervalue the work which volunteers do, whatever the level of skill or knowledge which it requires, is to belittle the people who are doing it. A volunteer to whom the purpose of a piece of work has been explained, who is convinced of its importance, and who understands the demands which it will make on him, may be stimulated to the extra effort required to meet these demands; or may realize that it would be impossible and withdraw. In either case the agency is better off than it would be with someone who had come in believing and expecting that not much would be required of him, and that no-one would be very much worse off if he gave up. This principle applies just as much to the simpler and more practical tasks as to those requiring skill and training. If work is not important, volunteers ought not to be asked to do it: if it is, they are entitled to know that their contribution matters and that they are relied upon to make it.

Selection

173   We have also sought information about methods of selection of volunteers, and the extent to which they are used, and find in this, as in other matters which we have studied, considerable diversity of practice. The degree and kind of selection used by any agency will naturally depend on the functions of the agency and the kinds of work for which volunteers are sought. There is an obvious difference between selecting volunteers for skilled and specialized work, and the kind of selection needed by bodies which recruit volunteers for a very

wide range of different services. The first type of agency can formulate its requirements, and then seek to develop methods of selecting the kind of people it needs; the second is recruiting for a number of services calling for various levels of ability, and will be concerned to exclude only those who seem unlikely to maintain the standards of the agency or to be suitable for any of the services concerned. Other types of agency, in their needs for selection procedures, come between these extremes.

Present Practice in Selection

174   In our questionnaire to voluntary organizations we asked them about their methods of selection and what proportion of volunteers they accepted. Of the 115 bodies whose replies were analysed, eighty-two said that they used some form of selection; and the great majority of these said that they accepted 75 per cent or more of those who volunteered. Other sources from which information was obtained included the survey of voluntary workers in Manchester and an investigation into the selection, placing and training of voluntary workers in Hampstead, which was carried out for the Camden Council of Social Service in 1965. In the Manchester report it is stated that relatively few of the seventy-seven statutory and voluntary bodies included in the survey had any formal selection procedures: while of twenty-four voluntary bodies questioned in the Camden survey, twenty-one said that they had no special method of selection.

175   The most rigorous selection procedures are found, as would be expected, in the specialist organization. Applicants for work as marriage guidance counsellors, after preliminary local selection, undergo a three-stage selection process, carried out at national level, consisting of an interview followed by two non-residential conferences. At the first of these conferences tests are given to gauge intelligence and attitudes: these are followed by further interviews, after which about 55 per cent of the original candidates remain. At the second conference a psychiatrist is present, and group discussions take place on situations with which counsellors might be faced. The propor-

tion of candidates eventually accepted as a result of the whole procedure is about 28 per cent.

176   Teamwork Associates, a project for recruiting and training volunteers for work with offenders, uses a training course as an important part of selection procedure. Applications are invited for the course, and those accepted for it (usually after a short interview) attend without any obligation or understanding that they will either enrol or be accepted as associates at the end of it. During the course, which takes place on one evening a week for seven weeks, the members learn what is expected of voluntary associates, and the demands which the work will make of them; and tutors are able to observe their reactions and attitudes. At the end, members are invited to apply for enrolment as associates, and usually about half of them do so. References are taken up, and each candidate is then interviewed by a selection panel. These interviews are fairly formal and rigorous, and in them the panel seeks to assess such factors as motives, relationships, maturity, values and attitude to authority. Usually about 80 per cent of those interviewed are accepted.

177   The National Citizens' Advice Bureaux Council gave us information about the procedures in a sample of twenty-three bureaux. Two of these said that they had no selection processes. The object of selection, as carried out by the remaining twenty-one, was to ascertain the candidates' suitability as regards temperament, intelligence, common sense, education; and their ability to respect confidence, to gain the confidence of clients and to work as members of a team. An interview was in all cases the main element in the selection process, but some bureaux also required completion of an application form and the giving of references. Most bureaux required attendance at a training course and a probationary period of work before final acceptance. The Survey of Organizers in Hospitals found that all organizers interviewed every prospective volunteer, including those recruited and sent by voluntary organizations, and regarded this as an important part of their work. The organizers in psychiatric hospitals often visited the homes of volunteers and interviewed them there, as they felt that this gave a better idea of

their personalities. Some organizers used application forms and some asked for references. One, who gave evidence personally to this Committee, said that she sometimes took up references, but as a rule relied on her personal judgment. If she considered that anyone sent by a voluntary organization would not be suitable for any work in the hospital she would ask the organization concerned to suggest something different for him. Most of the voluntary organizations which replied to our questionnaire relied on a single interview for the selection of volunteers, and the same procedure was used by sixteen of the seventy-seven organizations covered by the Manchester survey: only ten of the Manchester organizations used additional methods, requiring either a preliminary period of work or attendance at a training course before acceptance.

178   Of those organizations which said that they had no selection procedures some, for example the British Red Cross Society, felt that they needed volunteers for so many different kinds of work that something could be found to suit everybody; and some considered that no one offering voluntary service should be denied the opportunity to give it. Others thought that as the supply of voluntary workers always fell short of their requirements they could not afford to be selective. The Women's Royal Voluntary Service say it is their policy that all volunteers of good will shall, subject to references, be accepted by the Service, and selected thereafter for service within it. Sometimes a great deal of trouble is taken to find a suitable niche for a volunteer who seems unlikely to fit into any of the more usual kinds of work. Some organizations feel that it would be extremely difficult to reject any volunteer, and fail to see how they could tell people that they are not considered suitable for voluntary work. Others are convinced that people who are not suitable will find this out for themselves and withdraw altogether or look for different work. The Camden Council of Social Service asked voluntary bodies which said that they had no special method of selection what happened if the volunteers proved unsuitable: among the answers given were:

'Those unsuitable, after a trial, drop out.'

'We do not feel we can tell volunteers they are not wanted, even though they are really unsuitable.'

'In the rare event of a volunteer being unsuitable, they realise this themselves and leave.'

'Generally unsuitable ones either withdraw or are offered clerical work (this is usually not acceptable).'

Another organization told us that, although every volunteer was accepted, those considered unsuitable were put on a reserve list and never used. We consider that, in the interests of both clients and volunteers, agencies should be frank with those whom they believe to be unsuitable for their work.

The Place of Volunteer Bureaux in the Selection of Volunteers

179   Where there is an active volunteer bureau its work will necessarily include some degree of selection. It has to consider, in respect of any volunteer who seeks its help, what kind of work and what type of agency or organization to suggest; but it may occasionally be consulted by a would-be volunteer for whom, even though considerable efforts are made, it is not possible to suggest any suitable work. Sometimes a bureau, feeling that it would be too great a risk to pass on a volunteer of doubtful suitability, will offer work for a trial period within its parent organization. The primary function of the bureau is, however, to help the services rather than to assist individual volunteers, and to this end it has to develop methods of discovering the needs of local services, assessing the potentialities of volunteers, and matching the two. Some bureaux provide forms on which agencies needing voluntary workers are asked to give particulars of the help they require, describing both the work available for volunteers and the kinds of people they are seeking. Forms are also completed by the volunteers themselves, giving particulars of their personal circumstances, availability, experience, qualifications and interests. Such forms provide a useful foundation for the records of volunteers, the keeping of which is a necessary part of the work of a bureau. It must always be understood that a volunteer who is referred by a bureau to any

organization will not necessarily be accepted by it. The final decision must always rest with the organization in which he will be working, but bureaux will naturally be concerned to take whatever steps they can to avoid sending any volunteers on a succession of fruitless interviews.

180   Another function which bureaux might with advantage undertake to a greater extent than they appear to do at present, is to keep some continuing record of what happens to volunteers who have sought their advice and for whom work has been suggested. Such a record would be of general interest, would be a safeguard against volunteers becoming 'mislaid' or forgotten, and might be found useful by the bureaux themselves as an aid to evaluation of their methods of dealing with volunteers.

181   If there is no bureau it will fall to the agency which recruits the volunteer, or to which he offers his services, to carry out these functions, particularly if it is the type of organization which recruits volunteers for work in a large number of different services. More specialized agencies may also receive offers of help from people whom they are not themselves able to use, and in the absence of a bureau to which such people can be referred, the agency itself should endeavour to suggest other possibilities.

Allocation

182   Unless a volunteer is being sought for a special and individual piece of work, there will be a second stage of selection, or allocation to a particular job or type of work. This must be done within the agency in which he is working, and will be a function of the person responsible for the organization of voluntary work, probably in consultation with other staff with whom, or in whose department, the volunteer will be placed. Allocation and introduction to work overlap with, and cannot be separated from, preparation and training, which will be considered in the next chapter. Indeed, as we have seen, some organizations defer their final acceptance of a volunteer until

after a preparatory period of training or work. The choice of work for any volunteer need never be regarded as final and irreversible. It may be found that the first choice is not the best; or the volunteer himself, for reasons connected either with the work or with his personal circumstances, may wish to make a change. This may be arranged by the organizer of voluntary work in the agency for which he is working; or he may prefer to return to the bureau for advice about openings elsewhere. As the trend towards an increasing use of voluntary help and the training of volunteers for different and more skilled types of work continues, selection and allocation will assume even greater importance than they have at present. Just as much care is needed to fit people to the right job if they are volunteers as if they are paid workers; and this applies to the less demanding jobs as well as to those which require specialized skill.

Suggestions for the Future

183   We have not attempted to give detailed advice about methods of recruitment and selection. Some organizations may decide to experiment with different methods of recruitment themselves: others may seek professional advice on publicity. In some fields it has been found that to advertise specific types of need is effective: in others publicity about training courses has attracted recruits who might not have felt ready to commit themselves immediately to any kind of work, but were willing to learn. In general the subject is one about which there is little knowledge to draw upon. Many organizations have great experience and expertise in appealing for funds, but have not applied it to appealing for volunteers. Methods of selection, too, need to be more clearly thought out and more widely used; and the need to provide opportunities to move from one type of work to another should not be overlooked. Although continuity is valuable in voluntary work, as it is in many professional jobs, some degree of mobility may be an advantage both to volunteers themselves and to the services in which they work. It should be recognized that as the experience and skill of a voluntary worker increases he may need to move on to different and more demanding work. The selection and allocation of volunteers,

like their recruitment, are subjects about which there is still much to be learned. There is a need for the pooling of knowledge, for examination and assessment of existing methods, and for considerable further study and experiment.

Chapter 8

PREPARATION AND TRAINING

The Need For Training

184   Our terms of reference required us to give particular attention to the need of voluntary workers for preparation or training. We have found many indications that this need exists and is widely recognized, not least by volunteers themselves. We come now to consider what the requirements are and how volunteers can be helped through various forms of preparation and training to make their contribution as effective and satisfying as possible.

185   We discussed in the first instance whether the term 'preparation' should be used throughout this report as a substitute for 'training'. We were aware of fears that some volunteers might be discouraged by the idea that some sort of training course was an inevitable prelude to voluntary work of any kind; and that volunteers who had received training might begin to regard themselves, or be regarded by others, as having some kind of professional qualification. We think it possible to avoid these hazards, although it was not found possible to avoid the use of both terms. The word 'preparation' does not describe adequately the whole range of measures that may be taken to inform and equip volunteers. These include not only continuing guidance after introduction to the work, but also certain specific teaching processes which can properly be described as training. Both words have therefore been used, but it must be understood that what is here referred to as training is quite distinct from that required by social workers.

186   We shall examine the whole question in some detail. At this point we wish only to say that we believe every volunteer,

whatever he does, to be entitled to some degree of preparation for his work, so that he knows what the agency stands for and why his help is desired, has some idea of the kinds of people he will meet and what they expect of the agency and its voluntary workers, and is given opportunities to develop and direct his personal gifts and interests to the advantage of the work which he is doing. From the point of view of the agency using volunteers, the provision of some form of preparation is equally important. The agency needs to know the volunteer sufficiently well to have reasonable confidence in him and to believe that he will in fact do whatever he undertakes; to be able to rely on his understanding and acceptance of the agency's aims and standards; and to be sure that he is clear about matters such as the name of the person in the agency with whom he should keep in touch, or can consult, and practical details such as the refunding of expenses.

187   We consider that preparation of this nature is necessary for every volunteer. The majority will also find it helpful to have some background knowledge of community needs and the services that exist to meet them; while for certain types of voluntary work much more extensive training and continuing guidance are required. We shall discuss all these aspects of preparation and training later: here we have confined our comments to what we believe to be essential in order that every volunteer may have a good start. We believe that, as a result of this initial preparation or briefing, volunteers are likely to enjoy their work more and find it more rewarding. Those who proceed to further training appropriate to the work they undertake are likely, as a result of their greater knowledge and perception, to become increasingly acceptable to professional colleagues, administrators and clients; and thus inspire greater confidence in voluntary work generally.

The Present Position

188   Our examination of the provisions made at the present time for the preparation and guidance of volunteers has shown that the need for these is increasingly accepted. Of voluntary

organizations engaged in twenty-six major fields of work, half stated, in reply to an enquiry, that their volunteers were expected to take some form of training, and there has been an increase both in education about the social services and in training in certain specific fields of work. We also found, however, that these facilities appear to reach only a small proportion of volunteers and that most start their work with a minimum of introduction.

189   Courses which comprise general reviews of the social services and information about the people who use them are provided in many ways; by university extra-mural departments, adult education bodies, Councils of Social Service, the British Red Cross Society and other organizations. The lectures and courses offered are attended both by interested members of the public and by volunteers from different services. The range of information covered is wide but the approach is often rather formal and academic, and these courses can do little more than offer a means of extending their knowledge to that minority of the public prepared to seek information in this way. Courses of this kind may be of any length from a residential weekend to a course spread over a year. Speakers are usually drawn from the services described, or from a relevant university department or adult education body. In addition there may be a tutor, who provides some continuity throughout the course. These courses are probably less appropriate to the needs of the committed volunteer than to the general public; and their impact is likely to be considerably less than that of articles in the press and journals, and radio and television programmes, which reach a much wider public.

190   There are also some similar courses provided specifically for volunteers, but though they may be a little more focused, and discussion more informed, they are still too general to be more than a background to preparation for a particular task. They are useful in their way, and they are fully subscribed, fairly well attended, and apparently largely enjoyed but there are signs that their participants find them somehow unsatisfying, and certainly have difficulty in applying what they learn in them to the

practice of their work. There is a relatively frequent cry that not enough has been given, which probably means that the real, if undefined, need of the volunteer was not met. A more focused approach is attempted in talks or programmes on particular problems, clients or services, and these can provide volunteers engaged in those fields with a useful stimulus and starting point for discussion, and the opportunity to experience the reaction of others outside their immediate sphere of work.

191   Some discussions and seminars are being developed on an experimental basis with a view to enabling volunteers who may include people employed in various fields, to gain more understanding of problems of human behaviour. This approach, which may be found more demanding both by trainers and workers than more formal methods, is being used by certain organizations in which volunteers are involved in the more intensive personal services, and also in some of those relatively new fields where social workers are themselves still exploring ways of helping people who find it difficult to relate to others or to function in an established community.

192   Training in certain special skills, for example first aid and home nursing, is provided by the British Red Cross Society and the St John Ambulance Brigade, who offer certificates of competence in these subjects from elementary to advanced levels. Standards are agreed with the relevant professions, and examinations are set. These courses are attended not only by members of the organizations concerned, but by volunteers in other fields requiring such skills, or by members of the public wanting them for their personal interest or use. Training in other special skills is provided by individual organizations, for example beauty treatment for patients in hospital or at home by the British Red Cross Society, and maintenance of library services by the St John Ambulance Brigade. These are all forms of training, though provided at levels different from those of professional workers.

193   It is after the volunteer's offer of service has been accepted by an organization that his specific preparation or training

for his job begins, and even then he may share part of it with interested members of the public. For instance, courses about work with old people, offered by a number of Old People's Welfare Committees, may be attended by volunteers attached to those Committees, and also by volunteers, or occasionally by paid workers, working for local authorities or in old people's homes, as well as by members of the public. Such courses, relating to a particular field of work, provide the interested attender with an opportunity to obtain information about the subject, and can help a prospective volunteer to make up his mind before actually committing himself to work in this field.

194   There is considerable variety in the ways in which a new volunteer is introduced to his work. Most often his preparation starts with a talk (which may be part of a selection process) with a member of staff or experienced volunteer in the organization, giving him some idea of how his services can be used. This may be followed by a talk about the job itself, after which the pattern varies: he may be attached for a time to an experienced volunteer, may work in a group or team, or may immediately go off on his own to pay a visit or carry out some other piece of work. In a few organizations, such as some Settlements, the new recruit is left free in the first instance to meet other workers and attend any relevant meetings until he feels ready to embark on some particular work. Other organizations expect their recruits to attend several talks on the organization and its work, to read about it, or to work under supervision for a time. After starting work volunteers may subsequently have opportunities for discussion, or to attend meetings or conferences, but for a great many these opportunities rarely occur. Volunteers who are sent by their organizations to work in a hospital, residential home or other establishment, are often given further information on arrival, which may be very superficial or quite detailed and informative. It would be reassuring to be able to say that the amount and kind of information given to volunteers depends on, and is appropriate to, the demands of the task. It does in some measure relate to these, but it is clear that often the needs and potential of the job and of the worker have not been sufficiently thought out, and the opportunity to engage his interest fully is

often missed. Volunteers who had received some training are quoted by the Institute of Community Studies as saying: 'the lectures did not get down to the work as such', and, 'the course covered the subject but not the problems'.

195   There are many organizations which are aware of the need for greater care in preparing volunteers for their work but have not been able to mobilize resources to this end. Some of the national organizations have a recommended plan, but have difficulty in getting it applied equally at local level. This is a common problem of national bodies, and carries with it the danger that the national plan is geared to what is considered possible (and minimally necessary) for the less effective groups, thereby failing to give leadership at growing points in the organization.

196   The Committee's surveys showed that simple forms of briefing on the spot are reinforced in some organizations by occasional meetings, discussion groups, conferences or short courses for some workers, of a rather sporadic and unrelated nature. These show little evidence of careful assessment of need or maximum use of resources. They are often simply a means of getting administrative information across rather than providing opportunities for guidance, companionship and a sense of 'belonging'. This can be as true of national organizations with a plan, as of small local bodies.

197   There are some organizations in which a training policy has been worked out more fully, among them the British Red Cross Society and the St John Ambulance Brigade. All volunteers in Citizens' Advice Bureaux have an initial course of training. For part-time youth leaders two recent official reports have advised on a basic 'common element' training course, which is appropriate to the variety of settings and organizations in which adults undertake part-time youth work. Courses such as these are implemented at local level by joint statutory and voluntary training committees, or by local education authorities; and there is a Youth Service Information Centre, which has among its functions the development of relevant teaching

135

material. In both the Citizens' Advice Bureaux and Youth Service schemes the method of training is similar for both paid and unpaid part-time workers.

198   Elsewhere systematic attempts to train tend, understandably, to be in spheres where social workers or social work methods are closely involved, for example, some family counselling, and the care of offenders and their families. Here training, after initial procedures, is a continuing process, embodying the support, supervision and consultation which are essential in such demanding work. There are other fields of work, such as that of the Samaritans, in which the main effort is concentrated on providing in-service consultation, rather than on a preliminary course of training. In this way the volunteer can not only be supervised and supported, but can progressively gain understanding through discussion.

199   There are several influences at work affecting future patterns of preparation and training. The range of work undertaken by volunteers and the fields in which both they and social workers serve are constantly widening. In these new areas of work the volunteer is liable to find that he needs to know more, or to have closer contact with professional workers, so he seeks the collaboration of professionals (who may themselves be feeling their way in these new services) to devise ways of equipping himself. In so far as these volunteers demonstrate their capacity to undertake tasks not previously thought possible for them, or to provide new services to meet needs not previously tackled, they and their need for training and support are likely to be accepted. The training methods devised are likely to influence those now current in established voluntary services.

200   Another influence is brought to bear by the many volunteers who have careers of their own and who in the course of those careers have undergone training, have experienced work disciplines and have been accustomed to professional ethics and attitudes. These include many people trained in the profession of social work. Whilst in their voluntary work they may seek a different or less restricted sphere of activity, they appreciate

the need to apply themselves to a new task by acquiring knowledge and skill, in order to achieve a standard which will satisfy them. We believe that the contribution of such volunteers is of particular significance and value today.

201   Finally, those who undertake voluntary work before training as social workers, or before deciding whether to do so, can, through their awareness of the need for training, influence the pattern of what is provided. This influence needs to be treated with caution, as such people may be seeking something which will be a preliminary stage in their professional training, rather than what is needed by the majority of volunteers.

Arguments Against Preparation and Training and Some Answers

202   To many people the need for appropriate preparation or training for volunteers, and its advantages to the services, the clients and the workers themselves, is self-evident, but we have been presented with arguments against training by some organizations, professional workers and volunteers. Of the small sample of voluntary workers interviewed in the survey carried out by the University of Nottingham fewer than one in five claimed to have had any training, and only about one in eight of the remainder expressed any wish for it. It was concluded that: 'voluntary work in the social services is clearly seen as an unskilled activity demanding only personal characteristic qualities but not formal trainable skills'. The Institute of Community Studies found that of the seventy-four volunteers working in four of the services represented in their study sixty-seven had had no preparation or training, and three-quarters of these thought they did not need any, either because their work was simple and undemanding, or because they thought that common sense, maturity and experience of life were all that a volunteer needed. All the volunteers from the other two services included in this study, the Samaritans and Citizens' Advice Bureaux, had had some training, and agreed that it was necessary. An experienced School Care Committee worker said that in her experience there were some volunteers who desired training, but also many who did not want it at all. 'They like to

137

learn on the job, but they can flounder on this. They are often wise people, and can acquire the rest: they have neither the time nor the inclination for more.' The difficulty of finding time, both for the volunteers themselves and for those who would be responsible for providing training, was also mentioned by other witnesses. A group of workers from the British Red Cross Society were emphatic that for many jobs undertaken by volunteers no training at all was needed and perhaps no training would be useful. They thought that some workers, for example those helping in canteens, might resent the suggestion that they required training. The same fear, of objections by volunteers, was mentioned by some of the statutory and voluntary bodies which were consulted. Among the views expressed were that any attempt to impose training might cause them to lose potential workers, that training must be kept at a very informal level so as not to frighten members, and that volunteers would consider training unnecessary and boring.

203   We are of the opinion that much of this apparent resistance is due to the misleading and inappropriate use of the word 'training'. Certainly volunteers do not need to be 'trained' in any formal sense to carry out such tasks as delivering meals, making beds, or offering friendship. Appropriate briefing, however, which can give them increased understanding of how the service works, and show them how they can bring any unmet needs of their clients to the notice of those who may be able to help them, can increase the effectiveness of their work and their own satisfaction in doing it. Such briefing may also provide volunteers with opportunities which they would not otherwise have for meeting some of their fellow workers. Many of the volunteers who were consulted, engaged in a variety of different types of work, expressed the view that this type of preparation would be extremely valuable. The group of workers in clubs for psychiatric patients thought some professional workers were afraid that if they were given training they would become amateur psychiatrists, but they themselves felt that it would be helpful to have more information and opportunities for discussion with a social worker. 'You don't need training but someone to turn to for support and guidance.'

138

204   A rather different objection was that put forward in evidence from two of the associations of local authority officers. One of these stated that: 'services for which volunteers are recruited direct are not such as to call for training', while the other implied that in the view of some members training is not necessary because voluntary workers should not be used in work for which training is required. This objection is easily answered, since, as was shown in Chapter 5, volunteers are successfully undertaking work in many fields, including some local authority services, for which training is obviously necessary and is being provided. Indeed, we think it probable that the associations concerned would not now express their views in quite these terms.

205   Arguments about the time and expense likely to be incurred in training could be applied to any kind of develop-ment or expansion. If, as the Seebohm Committee found, and as we fully agree, there is a crucial role for volunteers in the social services, and if, as we also believe, their help cannot be properly effective unless they are given the support and assistance which suitable preparation or training and continuing guidance can provide, then it is just as necessary to devote some resources to this purpose as to the training of social workers. It must also be made clear from the outset to all volunteers that they will be expected to give some time to learning about their work. The amount will depend on the type of work they will be doing, the level of responsibility, and the degree of skill required.

206   Some social workers who thought training unnecessary, or even undesirable, seemed to fear that its effect might be to blur the distinction between volunteers and qualified workers: that both voluntary workers and administrators of the organiza-tions using them might consider that training would enable volunteers to take the place of social workers and to undertake skilled work without further guidance. There was also the fear that training, far from increasing the reliability and discretion of volunteers would have the opposite effect: workers who were known to have received training might be given too much

responsibility, or information about clients with which they were not equipped to deal, or which they could not be relied upon to treat confidentially.

207　There may well be some basis for these misgivings, but the answer to them is not to withhold training, but to ensure that it achieves its proper object of increasing the knowledge and effectiveness of voluntary workers. It should not only equip them to carry out their own tasks better, but should also give them some understanding of the functions and work of professional staff, and their accepted standards and ethics. Careful assessment of the kinds of preparation, training or guidance needed by volunteers in different services must take account of all these real or imagined dangers.

208　Finally there is the fear, sometimes explicitly stated, and sometimes implicit, particularly in statements about the special value and qualities of voluntary work, that training would impair the warmth, spontaneity and freedom of action which are so important and so highly valued. We believe there is a risk that unless training is planned and given by people who are fully aware of the nature of the volunteer's potential contribution something which is of real value may be lost in the process. This leads us to underline the importance of a practical approach to training, and of relating it both to the work to be done and to the people who will be doing it. Nor must we forget that some of the people best able to give the kind of guidance required may be found among experienced volunteers.

209　There is no magic about training, and there is no case for undertaking it for its own sake. It does not automatically benefit the volunteer, his client, his colleagues or his organization. It should be offered only to the extent that it is needed to enable the volunteer to develop his own potentialities, and to carry out the work which he has undertaken. Nor is it enough just to provide training. Steps should be taken to gauge the extent to which it is achieving its object, and it may be necessary to devise new ways of doing this.

General Education on Social Needs and Services

210   We have argued that volunteers need preparation or training to help them to give effective service, but there is also a widespread and fundamental need to increase general awareness by the public of social needs and services. The citizen should know about needs in the community, the services which endeavour to meet them, and where he might make some contribution himself. Any means which provide him with this awareness can be regarded as part of his general education, and of his equipment for everyday life. It could be said that the main and most valuable object of this part of general education is to enrich society by informing the individual citizen of the problems and needs of others, awakening his sympathy, providing him with an incentive to be helpful and to notice gaps or shortcomings, and informing him of the resources which may be available.

Schools

211   This consciousness of the needs of the community can first be fostered in schools, and we are glad to note that teaching on social needs and the provisions for meeting them is increasingly forming part of the curriculum. There is a growing tendency to link this study with direct observation of social services and participation in voluntary work. This is encouraged and discussed by the Schools Council in their working paper *Community Service and the Curriculum*. Here the subject is considered entirely from the point of view of the pupil and the school, with no adequate consideration of the clients. The Foreword comments that: 'if schools feel that their pupils should know of the needs and troubles of their community at first hand they will treat that community as a normal part of curricular activity'. The paper goes on to justify the use of community service in terms of broad educational requirements and asks: 'what, in concrete terms has it to offer the teacher in the classroom?' It says that community service: 'can only usefully serve curricular purposes if it is timetabled', and that unless it 'can be taken account of in the examinations most pupils will

remain blind to its opportunities'. It is reasonable that the main concern of educators should be education, and one headmaster is quoted as saying that the community service work in school time is the generator that gives momentum to what goes on out of school. However, it would seem less acceptable if the success or failure of any piece of work were judged by its effect on the child, without any reference to the client: one teacher is quoted as saying: 'a small minority of girls and boys contributed little to the scheme but we believe they benefited from association with the many who did'.

212   We would not dispute that one of the best ways of learning about people's needs and the services provided for them is by direct observation and experience. Such observation and experience form an essential part of the training of social workers, but there are difficulties about providing similar opportunities for school children. There is not at present a great demand by schools for visits of observation to people in need; but if such visits were to become routine for most children as part of their education there would be a danger of the users of the social services being subject to unwarrantable intrusion for the benefit of the children and without any advantage to themselves. The social services must give priority to the needs of their clients, and cannot see them regarded primarily as teaching material. We are convinced that teachers with imagination can find ways, other than by direct observation or participation, of presenting vividly to children the needs of people and the working of the social services.

213   We are also concerned about the effects on children themselves of being involved in community service, not because they have freely chosen to do something in their own time to help other people but because it is part of their school work. We recognize that a school, as a corporate body, may become concerned with some problem in the community, and that children may wish to make a contribution, but to include community service in compulsory education, or to do more than encourage spontaneous participation by children not only negates the concept of service but may defeat its own aims. Quite apart from

our doubts as to the value of 'service' of this kind to the people who receive it, we fear that children may come to look on it as a part of their school life which most of them will automatically shed when they leave school.

214   There is no lack of evidence that children do offer service of many kinds voluntarily and in their own time; and we are aware of the imaginative ways in which some schools stimulate interest in social service and encourage the desire to serve. It is because this spontaneous giving of help is so important and so much to be valued that we are nervous about the introduction of any element of compulsion. Our anxiety is increased by the extent to which community service as a school subject is advocated as something which will benefit the children, and not primarily because it is seen to have advantages for the rest of the community. Schools seek opportunities for service by children but we are doubtful whether enough thought is always given to whether the services which they offer are needed, or can appropriately be undertaken by very young volunteers whose assistance is likely to be available for only a limited period. For all these reasons we have very considerable reservations about the guidance given by the Schools Council, and the encouragement by education authorities of community service as an educational activity within the curriculum; and about the expressed desire of at least one of the organizations providing opportunities for service by young people to see it enormously increased.

Further and Adult Education

215   Young people who, after leaving school, want to bring their knowledge up to date, or to explore the subject more fully, can be catered for between the ages of 15 and 18 through liberal studies courses in colleges of further education. Probably Liberal Studies Departments could pay more attention to this field than they do at present. In adult education, provided by university extra-mural departments, by bodies such as the Workers' Educational Association, and by local education authorities in evening institutes and daytime non-vocational

143

classes, courses on the social services should become far more widely available, and should appear in each year's programme. Interested members of staff in Social Studies Departments of universities and colleges of further education could often take more initiative in promoting such courses or in making known their readiness to advise and help with courses initiated in other ways. Both statutory and voluntary social service organizations could assist by drawing the attention of educational bodies to the need for courses, by advising on their form and content, and by publicizing those which are arranged. If there is difficulty in finding teaching staff there may be a need for some short courses of training to enable more teachers, and probably experienced volunteers, to play a part.

216   These general introductory courses must reflect the wide range of interest in the community in this subject. There is a need for a continuing basic theme, and for its development. There should also be experiments in scope and presentation, and continued evaluation as these experiments are applied and adapted. It is important that the courses should be flexibly planned, to be able to suit their particular audiences and to be adapted to changing circumstances and shifts in the focal points of public information and concern.

217   Topics of social concern have an important place in the mass media, radio, television and the press, which is probably a reflection of the spreading interest in social problems. We should like to see an expansion of these programmes, with more informed and systematic planning, relating topical dramas and crises to the wider context of need and provision. The radio programme 'Helping Your Neighbour', a series of talks and discussions on voluntary work which was produced in an afternoon series early in 1969, and in which volunteers, social workers and clients took part, was a very welcome contribution. Further programmes of this kind would be useful, and of considerable interest to a wider audience than is able to listen to a programme broadcast in mid-afternoon. The participation of the Schools Broadcasting Council, and the other Education and Further Education Advisory groups to the different broadcasting

companies, could clearly be of immense value in developing and piloting some experimental projects. On these they would, no doubt, obtain advice from bodies concerned with particular services. The Open University might also be able to make an important contribution.

Relating the Content of Preparation and Training to the Needs of the Volunteer

218   The preparation or training provided for a volunteer is designed to equip him to carry out specific work for which paid workers are either not indicated or not available, or for which the particular contribution of a volunteer is more appropriate. The training of volunteers has aims which are different from those of professional social work training, but this does not mean that it can afford to be less than appropriate. If it is, there is loss, either because money and time are spent on training uselessly or unnecessarily or because the volunteer is not used to his full capacity. The training of social workers aims to give them a considerable body of knowledge about human relationships and the structure and function of society. It is designed to enable them to acquire skills which they can adapt to work with a wide range of clients in a variety of services. The skills required by some volunteers, particularly those who are working in a close personal relationship, are more narrowly focused to the particular job in hand. Other volunteers may tackle a range of different but less complex problems, or may move from one task of this kind to another, and their work is distinguished from that of social workers by its different level of involvement. The kind of work the volunteer is to undertake is a primary factor in determining what preparation or training he needs, though it is possible to indicate certain general requirements for three broad but not necessarily exclusive categories of work, namely work which is mainly of a practical kind, work based on personal relationships with individuals and their families, and work with groups.

219   Volunteers whose work is to be primarily of a practical kind such as providing transport, serving refreshments in a club

or clinic, helping in a clothing store or assisting with gardening, decorating or household tasks, usually have some knowledge or experience of the type of work they are undertaking. They may need simply to be shown how to adapt this to any special situation and to the requirements of the organization to which they are attached. Knowledge of the aims of the organization and how it functions will help them to realize that they are not working in isolation but are part of a service which can offer them advice and help if they need it or if they become aware of problems with which they are not equipped to deal. In so far as their work will bring them in contact with clients, they will also need to have some broad understanding of them and their needs, and why they require help.

220   Volunteers who will be involved in close personal relationships, whether their work is the befriending of a lonely person or is concerned with helping people who have complex problems, will need above all to know something of human reactions and behaviour. They may need help in understanding the feelings and attitudes of clients and in realizing that the relationship has to be one of mutual acceptance. They need to learn something of the arts of communication and establishing relationships, of how to give and receive information and respect confidence. It is important, too, that they should be able to judge how far they can go in dealing with a difficult situation, and when and where to turn for advice and help. A general background knowledge of the needs of the community and the services which exist to meet them will be of particular value to these workers, whose clients may be involved with a variety of services.

221   Those who work with people in any kind of residential care, or in groups such as clubs will need to acquire an understanding of relationships within groups and communities. They will also need to know something of the organization responsible for the setting in which they are working, its functions and policies. Awareness of the need for participation by members of a group has to be fostered and an understanding of how and when groups can be helped to become less dependent and more

146

self-directing. A capacity for organization and leadership may also be required.

222   The emphasis in the preparation or training needed by any volunteer will depend on which of these elements, practical help, personal relationships with individuals or families, or with those in residential settings or in groups, predominates in the work which he is undertaking. In planning training it will be necessary to bear in mind not only the demands which the work will make on the volunteer, but also his own experience, capacity, and attitudes, and the resources which are available for training and continuing guidance or support. The amount of information, skill or awareness which volunteers may need to acquire will depend on these factors, and will vary greatly, but it is essential that each volunteer should be helped to see how his learning can be applied to his own work. Any training scheme which fails to enable him to apply his knowledge can achieve little, and may even defeat its aim by confusing him or undermining his confidence.

223   There are various ways in which the training needed to fit a particular volunteer for his task can be planned and developed. It might, for example, be found helpful in the first instance to consider and tabulate the various factors required in any task, and we give below some suggestions which may serve as a guide. Some of the requirements mentioned here would be applicable to any category of work; some relate to particular categories; and some are more specialized skills, obviously not needed by all volunteers but appropriate for those selected for responsibility and leadership:

(1) Information
  (a) Such knowledge as may be necessary or helpful regarding the place of the specific field of work in the general network of community services; and information about other related services which may be enlisted to meet the needs of clients.
  (b) Information about the particular service to which the volunteer is, or is to be, attached, its organization,

147

methods of working and traditions; about professional workers in this field, their aims, responsibilities and professional ethics.

(c) Information about characteristics of the people for whom this service is intended; and about the attitude of society towards these people, as exemplified by its actions, laws and provisions.

(d) Information regarding the volunteer's own work and the terms and conditions of his service; for example, to whom he is responsible, minimum period of commitment, payment of expenses, insurance.

(e) Specific information such as is needed by workers in Citizens' Advice Bureaux, volunteer bureaux, or other information services.

(2) Skill

(i) practical and organizational
(ii) concerned with communication and relationships

(i) (a) Practical skills such as cooking, handicrafts, painting and decorating;

(b) home nursing; helping the physically handicapped;

(c) record keeping and report writing, including keeping notes of meetings;

(d) planning and evaluation of a service; public relations;

(e) teaching and training skills.

(ii) (f) relating to people by interviewing them in an agency, talking to them in their own homes, or visiting them in residential establishments;

(g) working with groups;

(h) gaining the co-operation of officials and others whose help is required on behalf of clients.

(3) Understanding

(a) understanding a client's feelings;
(b) understanding community attitudes;
(c) understanding the volunteer's own attitudes.

224   These three groups of requirements exemplify the three elements of knowledge, skill and understanding, strands which

interweave in all patterns of training, though sometimes one and sometimes another will predominate. From a schedule of this kind (amplified as may be found necessary) those who are planning a scheme of preparation and training might select the requirements applicable to the work which the volunteer or group of volunteers will be undertaking, and from these develop a plan, in accordance with the needs of the volunteers and the resources available. We believe this schedule can provide a basis from which the simplest as well as more elaborate schemes could be developed.

225   The volunteer's own qualities and attitudes are likely to be a most important aspect of his contribution, particularly where, as in supporting, befriending and counselling roles, it is through them that he must work. These qualities and attitudes, together with the reasons which underlie his taking up voluntary work, will have a bearing on the preparation which he will require, and it may be necessary for him in this preparation, to acquire some awareness of his own motives. Motives are of greater significance in some kinds of work than in others, and have positive as well as negative aspects, though the latter tend to attract most notice. Motives deriving from experience of disability or loneliness, seeking a means to a career, and other personal circumstances can have positive value. With training and continuing guidance it is often possible to make constructive use of other motives, which are sometimes frowned upon, such as underlying feelings of guilt or conflicts regarding authority, provided that the volunteer is helped to some awareness and acceptance of these feelings. For instance, those who are or have been mentally ill often feel an urge to help others, and this may be part of what they see as their own need. If they are able to gain the necessary measure of detachment they may have particularly good insight and understanding to bring to their work. It should not be forgotten that professional workers have similar motives, though their longer training provides more opportunity to deal with them. Just as it is necessary to consider motivation in selecting students for training as social workers, so careful selection of volunteers should help to eliminate those who have problems which are likely seriously to affect their work.

226   It must be borne in mind that in some situations the demands on the volunteer may change as the task progresses. For instance, the needs of the client may change, or he may come to regard the volunteer differently. A client in the early stages of adaptation to disability or bereavement, or on first returning to the problem of living outside hospital or prison, or of living in a new country and culture, may be, and need to be, considerably dependent on the volunteer. As the client settles down, he will need to achieve a greater degree of independence and it will be the task of the worker to help him to do this. The preparation of the volunteer should make him aware of the likelihood of such changes and developments, and able to adjust his method of working to meet the changes as they arise.

Methods of Preparation and Training

227   Various factors need to be taken into account in considering methods of preparation and training. There are predisposing factors in volunteers which influence the training method, for example, readiness to learn, educational attainments, and attitude to the role of learner. As the range of backgrounds from which volunteers are drawn is extended, we see a need for less formal and more imaginative teaching methods, and those used by trade unions, as well as management, in the industrial field, may be helpful. On the other hand, as general levels of education change and new methods are introduced in schools, universities and colleges, so will a readier response be found among volunteers to imaginative learner-centred methods. Similarly, changes in the level of knowledge among volunteers, resulting from improved general education about the social services, will call for changes in the content of training, and may allow its aims to be extended. Development and advance in teaching methods, however, proceed with varied pace in different settings. Those concerned with the training of volunteers may be either richer or poorer in imaginative ideas about method than the educational bodies in their area. There is urgent need for the building up of a body of information, experience and expertise. It would be particularly important to explore the possibilities of more practical and less theoretical methods to

help the less academic volunteer; and to study such questions as how to make the best use of training time, how to overcome problems arising from irregular geographical distribution of volunteers and from shortages of trainers and educators, and how to encourage volunteers to undertake some of their training at home, if they cannot be available for training elsewhere.

228   A volunteer's training can include private study and individual or group tuition. It may be concentrated within a short space of time or spread over a long period. It can take place in his own home, at the place where he is working, or at residential or non-residential gatherings of workers, which may include paid staff as well as volunteers. The training can be a distinct process, whether preliminary, concurrent with work, or refresher; or it may be part of the process of continuing support and guidance which is discussed in the following section. Numerous factors will influence the pattern of training for the volunteer. Some of them will depend on the resources of the agency—what people and what funds are available to facilitate training, and at what times. Other factors will be connected with the volunteer's attitude towards training, and his availability. Still other factors, and in an ideal world these would be the overriding ones, would be the training needs of the volunteer in relation to his projected service.

229   As we suggested earlier, training should include the three elements of knowledge, skill and understanding. This means that the volunteer needs opportunities for learning facts, principles and concepts, in the light of which he will act; he needs to practise his work, either in real or in simulated situations; and to discuss and reflect on his own interaction with others, in order to enlarge his own awareness of himself and his effect on other people. The relative proportions of these three elements will clearly differ according to the training needs to be met and the other factors (the availability of the volunteer for training and of training resources) referred to above.

230   In putting into effect this kind of training programme, the tutor will make full use of what is known about how people

learn; for example, that active participation by a learner is preferable to passive reception, and that teaching tends to be most productive when presented as problem-solving tasks. There may be need for further study and consideration of how older people can best be helped to acquire new knowledge and skill. The tutor will select whichever method or combination of methods is most appropriate. When the accent is on conveying basic factual information or knowledge, didactic methods are likely to be more in evidence, though not by any means dominant. Thus, lectures, films, visits of observation and similar aids to learning, used as relevantly and imaginatively as possible, are likely to be more appropriate for the development of knowledge than for the other two elements. There will also be a place for active discussion, to enable principles and their implications to be absorbed, and to show how the information which is presented can be applied to practical problems.

231   In helping volunteers to acquire skill, whether it is of a mainly practical kind or concerned with communication and relationships, the emphasis will be on practice. This can be provided by such means as role playing, presentation of dummy cases, and supervised experience. Discussion of experience and of case material will have an important place; and films or books which describe practice may be found useful. There may also be lectures or talks by an experienced worker, volunteer or otherwise, who is familiar with the kinds of situation in which the volunteers concerned may find themselves.

232   In order to develop understanding, discussion is likely to be the most important method. The material provided for discussion can be focused on some particular problem; for example, on loneliness in general and on specific examples of it. Members of a group will present various attitudes which can be discussed, questioned and confirmed or otherwise. Volunteers will be able to draw upon their own experience in other spheres, and will learn through becoming more aware of their own attitudes and those of the rest of the group. The main function of the tutor in these discussions will be to provide comments or explanations when they are required. Later in this chapter we

make some suggestions as to how the resources needed for the provision of training might be increased and made more readily available.

Supervision and Guidance on the Job

233 Supervision, in ordinary usage, denotes the kind of oversight given by a responsible person to the work of someone with less responsibility, in order to ensure that a task is being adequately performed. A supervisor may simply need to be satisfied that a person who is carrying out a straightforward piece of work has the necessary ability and is sufficiently careful and reliable, or may require from time to time to give some practical help, advice or instruction. In social work practice the word has been adopted to denote the process through which support, guidance and increasing insight are gained by students and less experienced staff; and which can also be helpful to experienced social workers. It can be applied in much the same sense to the guidance which is required by many voluntary workers; and we are using it in this sense though we have some objections to the term, because we believe that it will be generally understood and we have been unable to find a satisfactory alternative.

234 Supervision is particularly necessary for volunteers whose work involves relationships with individuals. In social work its most important object is the provision of support and continuing training so that workers may develop good standards of practice with the minimum risk of damage to clients. For volunteers, who lack the basic professional knowledge acquired by social workers in their training, experience on the job and observation of the work of others are important educators, but the responsible organization has a duty to ensure that education of this sort is not gained at the expense of the client. Therefore these learning experiences must be guided by a more experienced worker. The training of a volunteer is not completed after one short course, but must be a continuing process, with differing degrees of intensity and emphasis, and supervision is thus one of the most important elements. It can also be a means of en-

abling organizations, and those who are supervising volunteers, to assess what is possible for a volunteer in a given situation, and so, while aiming at high standards, to avoid making excessive demands on the workers.

235   At first sight it may seem surprising, in view of the weight of opinion given to the need for supervision and support of volunteers, that there is so little evidence of its provision or of any serious attempt to undertake it. This may be because organizations have an unrealistic faith in the unaided efforts of their workers, or because, although they have good intentions, they fail to put them into effect; possibly too as a result of the tendency to use voluntary workers in situations of strain and overwork. It may also be because the use of volunteers in work which may present complex problems is a fairly recent development. If techniques of evaluation of services or assessment of consumer opinion were better developed and more widely used in this field they might bring to light many shortcomings in the effectiveness of services, the use of resources available, and the satisfaction of both clients and workers, which could be attributed to the failure to supervise or to give adequate support.

236   Supervision, which may often be undertaken by suitably experienced voluntary workers, is provided through the giving of advice, information or constructive criticism, but perhaps most effectively through discussions, in which the voluntary workers concerned, as well as supervisors, have an active part to play. These discussions may relate to facts, principles or policy, to special problems encountered by workers, or to the needs of individual clients, and here we see again the same three elements, knowledge, skill and understanding. Sometimes supervision is almost continuous, as when a volunteer is working directly with a social worker; or it may be given through regular and frequent consultation, or by sporadic and infrequent contact. The amount and degree of guidance and support required will depend on the type of work undertaken by the volunteer, the extent of his responsibility, and his own capacity and experience. Some volunteers may require frequent professional guidance, with opportunities for consultation with experienced

154

paid or voluntary workers. Others, whose work does not normally bring them into touch with complex problems, may need only to keep their supervisors informed of what they are doing, and know that advice is available for them whenever they need it.

237   Although there has been criticism of volunteers on the grounds that they fail to appreciate the need to report back or to consult, this appears to be untrue of those who have any experience of the benefits of consultation and discussion, and some hope of obtaining them. Evidence of present provisions shows that in the majority of services it is left entirely to volunteers, even from the early stages, to seek guidance only when they feel it to be needed, and they are often quite uncertain where to turn. Evidence also shows that when continuing guidance is offered most volunteers welcome it as meeting a need of which they are very conscious, and they do not generally regard the process of evaluation of their work with suspicion. It is important that this should be so, and that volunteers should be encouraged to talk about their work, to ask questions, and to say when they do not understand what is happening. In the early stages the supervisor will probably need to take the lead in guiding a discussion and bringing out relevant issues, but as time goes on the volunteer is likely to become more aware of the matters he needs to raise, and to play a more active part in discussion.

238   The role of the supervisor or consultant has many aspects. He is a channel of information between the worker in the field and policy makers: he may have administrative responsibilities and a part to play in the planning of training, for he should know what training his volunteers have received and be in a position to judge of its efficacy. He is also concerned in the important business of fitting the volunteer to a suitable job and so to the appropriate client. There are some supervisors who sustain all these roles, but it may be necessary for a number of different people to be involved in the carrying out of different aspects. Some organizations will have workers, paid or voluntary, who are ready to take on these functions, or who could do so after some special training, but it may be that experienced

supervisors will have to be recruited from outside: in this case another task for the supervisor might be the in-service training for supervisory work of suitable individuals within the organization. It will be necessary to consider in which situations supervision by a social worker is required. It is not by any means always a necessity, but now that professional workers of many kinds are working more and more with volunteers, they are increasingly involved in some measure in consultation and supervision.

239   The task of supervision with its particular responsibilities requires special qualities and is not congenial to all workers, whether professionals or volunteers, many of whom prefer the demands and rewards of direct personal service to the client to responsibility for other workers and its attendant problems. The supervisor, though it is part of his job to encourage the volunteer to take initiative and assume responsibility, may, in the nature of things, have to be answerable to a considerable extent for the work which is undertaken. He must also take into account the fact that the professional and contractual obligations to which social workers are subject do not necessarily apply to voluntary workers. He has, in fact, to carry a considerable burden. Moreover, the greater the demands on the volunteer, and particularly the demands on his personal qualities and his understanding of his work, the greater will be his demands on the supervisor. From this it follows that there are varying limits to the number of volunteers for whom any supervisor can take responsibility. It is likely, although other elements enter in, that the more personal the work the fewer this number will be.

240   It must be recognized that changes may take place in the life and personal relationships of a volunteer during, or because of his voluntary work, as may be the case with any other worker. There may also be situations in which a volunteer dealing with other people's problems is brought face to face with problems of his own for which he may need help. He may consciously or unwittingly expose his personal problems, and the supervisor needs to be alert to such situations and decide to what extent he should allow himself to become involved. He

must be prepared to help the volunteer to contain and resolve some of his problems where they are not disabling and can be used constructively, but he has to limit his involvement to discussion of that part of the problem which intrudes on the volunteer's work. If more than this is required he must steer the volunteer to the more specialized help he needs. Nor is this a problem exclusive to volunteers: it is a staff relationship problem which occurs in many other contexts, but it is important to volunteers in that they may, like other workers, be using their work to try to bring about a balance in their own lives.

241   Difficulties may also arise through the differing expectations which volunteers have of what training will be and what it will do for them. They may react differently to the demands which training makes on them: some feel that too much is asked, and others that they are not doing or getting enough. If problems of this kind are not to impede the volunteer they may need to be resolved by discussion.

Further Training

242   Volunteers are usually anxious to begin to do some useful work as quickly as possible. They do not, like professionals, expect to have to complete a long course of training first; nor, as a rule, do they find it easy to spare much time for it. Their preparation and initial training tend, therefore, to be of fairly short duration and focused on the demands of a particular job or type of work. It is, therefore, especially important that there should be facilities not only for supervision and discussion of their work, but also for further training for those who wish to increase their knowledge and widen their understanding. There is a place for short courses of various kinds, day or week-end conferences, seminars and discussion groups. These may be concerned with general principles, or with particular areas of work, and may be designed for volunteers only, or open also to paid workers. They may provide opportunities for meeting and discussion both between people doing similar work, with similar problems and experiences; and between those working in very different fields, who may yet find much that is of common interest. We have referred earlier to what is already being done

in these directions, both by co-ordinating bodies such as Councils of Social Service and by some specialized agencies which regard activities of this kind as an essential part of their training programmes. In general, however, such developments are still far too sporadic and need to be much more closely related to problems which volunteers are actually meeting, and to needs of which they themselves are conscious.

243   There will also be a need for short courses of a rather more advanced kind for volunteers, as well as paid workers, who will act as organizers or trainers. In paragraph 159 we mentioned some of the factors required in training courses for organizers. The report of King Edward's Hospital Fund on organizers in hospitals makes more detailed suggestions; and mentions the need for organizers to be well informed not only on all that is involved in dealing with volunteers, but also on the structure and purpose of the statutory social services, of voluntary organizations, and of trade unions in the National Health Service. Some of these matters may be covered in courses provided for volunteers undertaking other work, or in general educational courses; but it will be necessary to relate what is learned in such courses to the functions of the organizer in particular services. Courses for trainers have been provided for some time by certain voluntary organizations, such as the British Red Cross Society and the National Old People's Welfare Council, but the role of trainer does not appear to have been very clearly defined. In paragraphs 251 to 253 we give our views on the functions of trainers and their own need for training. The emphasis for them is not so much on direct teaching skill as on ability to assess what it is that volunteers need to learn, and how this can best be presented to them. The trainer must take account not only of the requirements of the service with which he is concerned, but also of the capacity, availability and attitude to training of the volunteers.

Co-ordination of Training

244   Although preparation and training for voluntary workers are increasing, the impact is still far too limited; and

there are very large numbers of volunteers whom it does not reach at all. We are of the opinion that more training facilities are needed, but that an even more pressing need at this stage is for proper co-ordination. We have seen that preparation and training include many stages and processes, and that for some workers preparation merges into consultation and supervision, all being related to the needs of the individual volunteer and the demands of the work which he is doing. In most areas of work, however, there is a place for a planned course of training, as part of the whole process, and we have found that existing courses fall into the following broad categories:

(a) General background courses about social needs and ser-
    vices.
(b) Courses specifically intended for workers in the social
    services, but of a fairly general type.
(c) Training provided by individual organizations for their own
    workers who will be undertaking specialized work.

Examples of these three types are given in Appendix IV. To some extent they correspond with the three elements in training which we have already mentioned, in that the emphasis in course of type (a) is on imparting information; in type (b) on helping people to acquire skill; and in type (c) on developing understanding.

245   Our view, as we have already indicated, is that courses of type (a) should be generally available to people of all ages, not necessarily as preparation for any kind of social service, but as an important part of their general education. We consider that the statutory and voluntary bodies which use volunteers should not be expected to draw on their own resources to provide teaching of this kind, but that it should be provided by the education services. In paragraphs 215 and 216 we have suggested some ways in which its provision might be extended, and the courses themselves made more useful. Agencies using volunteers will be concerned to stimulate the provision by educational

159

bodies of general background courses and to make use of them, when appropriate, for their workers.

246   Organizations which use voluntary help will also need to consider the specific preparation or training needed by volunteers in the services with which they are concerned, whether what is required is fairly simple briefing, discussion of principles, the learning of skills applicable to various types of work, or specialized training. It is here that co-operation between agencies, and joint planning, would be of the greatest value, but such co-ordination appears at present to be rare. One example of present arrangements is found in the survey of the preparation and training of voluntary workers in Manchester where, of the 77 organizations covered by the survey, 50 provided individual briefing, 50 arranged meetings, and 23 said that their volunteers had attended courses. These included the regular courses in first aid and home nursing and, in addition, particulars were given of nineteen other courses for voluntary workers, provided by fourteen of the Manchester organizations. The length of these courses ranged from one-day schools to a course of fifty-six lectures spread over nine months. With very few exceptions, they were run by particular organizations for volunteers who were already working for them, or intended to do so. Some of these agencies said that they had consulted 'outside bodies' about their courses, but the survey comments that: 'in general the picture was of relatively little outside consultation on training'.

247   In London, courses for voluntary workers have been arranged by the London Council of Social Service, but for some years these were exclusively for those working with old people. During the last four or five years, however, a few courses have been provided for volunteers from a number of different services and types of work. The first of these was attended by thirty-one people from eighteen different organizations, not selected in any way, but subsequently there has been some experiment with courses for selected groups, for example people doing various kinds of work involving relationships with individual clients. We were informed that it was hoped to increase the number of these 'generic' courses.

248　　It is recognized that the training provided at present by some organizations is guided by national policies, and that, in the first instance, some such bodies, or others which undertake specialized work, might find it difficult to accept that any of their training programmes could be shared. Even so, it is to be hoped that such bodies would be prepared to co-operate in discussion and planning, and to make their advice available to others which have less experience. Many agencies consider it important that volunteers should identify themselves strongly with their particular organization, and some think that this identification and involvement can best be achieved by providing all training initially within the agency. Although we have some sympathy with this point of view, we do not agree that a volunteer's involvement with and loyalty to his agency are likely to be seriously jeopardized if he shares appropriate parts of his training with workers from other services. In general it is to be expected that a good deal of co-operation between agencies would be found possible in providing the kinds of training offered in courses of types (b) and (c) referred to above (paragraph 244), and also in arranging seminars or discussion groups, or short courses and conferences for volunteers who have had some training and experience.

Local Joint Committees

249　　There is a need everywhere for some local body, representative of statutory and voluntary agencies, to consider, advise on, and co-ordinate training for volunteers in all services. In most parts of the country such a body might conveniently cover a county, together with any county boroughs within its boundaries; but there is room for considerable flexibility in determining the areas to be covered. This body, which we refer to as the Joint Committee for the Training of Voluntary Workers, would need to seek the co-operation and representation of educational bodies, and would also, no doubt invite the churches to be represented. The Committee would survey the available resources for training, both in the educational field and in the agencies themselves; and also the requirements of all organizations using or wishing to use volun-

L　　　　　　　　161

tary help. It would discuss how the best use could be made of existing resources, and how facilities for training could be improved. It would seek to identify common elements in the training requirements of different services; considering, for example, whether courses could be devised which would meet the needs of people who undertake home visiting for a number of agencies, for people engaged in club or other group activities, or for those undertaking counselling and casework services. It would be in a position to stimulate and advise on the provision of suitable educational courses on the social services, as well as concerning itself with actual training. It would be the local focus for all matters relating to the training of volunteers and, once established, would have an important function as a base for the discussion of related subjects such as recruitment and selection. The initiative in setting up such a Committee might be taken by a local authority or by a Council of Social Service or by some other voluntary body which recognized the need for a development of this kind. In view of the interest expressed by government departments in the extension of voluntary work, the departments concerned might well be prepared to give official encouragement.

A National Focus

250   Local Committees of the kind suggested would almost certainly feel a need for some national focus or co-ordinating body, and this need could be met by the establishment of a central foundation, concerned with training and the many other aspects of voluntary work in the social services. We shall consider the structure and functions of such a foundation in Chapter 10. Among the many ways in which it could contribute to the development of training would be by the study, description and evaluation of methods; advice on syllabuses; the provision of, or advice on, training for supervisors, organizers or trainers of voluntary workers; arrangement of conferences and short courses. It should be a source not only of information and advice, but also of energy; not only a co-ordinating body, but one which plays an active part in stimulating development and experiment.

The Trainers

251   At the local level each agency should have some person to be generally responsible for the promotion of training and for liaison with the local Joint Committee. In Manchester it was found that, although only a minority of the seventy-seven organizations included in the survey had systematically planned training, the great majority had some person or persons who were regarded as having the main responsibility for it. In twenty-eight of the organizations this work was undertaken by staff who in some cases were qualified social workers; and in thirty-two by volunteers. Seven organizations used both staff and volunteers, and ten gave no information. These seventy-seven organizations had, between them, over 7000 volunteers, and the people responsible for the training of over 4000 of them were themselves voluntary workers. They included many who had had considerable experience, and some who had had specific training for this part of their work. Those who had had special training were for the most part people working for branches of national organizations such as the British Red Cross Society, the British Legion and the Women's Royal Voluntary Service. In the main, responsibility for training rested with people who had relevant experience in the social services, rather than any particular qualification for training others, and we would expect this example to be broadly representative of the general position.

252   In any agency the choice of the person who is to be responsible for ensuring that volunteers obtain the necessary preparation or training, at whatever level it may be required, is an important one. In some agencies this responsibility may rest with the organizer of voluntary work; in others, the person selected may be some other member of the staff or an experienced volunteer. This person will be involved in some of the actual processes of preparation or training, in preliminary briefing, in consultation or supervision, in tutoring courses, seminars or discussion groups, or in actual teaching of a rather more formal kind. The main function with which we are concerned here, however, is that of assessing the needs of the agency and

163

of its individual volunteers for preparation or training of any kind, and finding the best ways of meeting them, with the help of educational bodies and in co-operation, as far as may be possible, with other local agencies. The person who is to do this may himself require help and guidance. He will need, among other things, to understand not only all the functions of his own agency, but something of the work of others. There will be obvious advantages in arrangements by which such people, from different agencies, can meet one another from time to time, to discuss general aspects of training, and the interrelation of their respective needs. The local Joint Committee would be an appropriate body to arrange such meetings or conferences.

253   It will, no doubt, be found that there are many people in the social and educational services whose help can be called upon in carrying out plans for training. Some of them are already involved to a considerable extent, and there are many busy people who are asked to spend too much of their time in giving talks about the services which they represent to small, unrelated groups of volunteers. Such talks are usually directed in some degree to the interests of the particular audience, but a great deal of their content is, or could be, common ground. Both paid and voluntary workers who are engaged in the training of volunteers are likely to benefit from advice and discussion, both of methods and of content; and it may be found that the provision of some kind of training for these people is a priority. This would be one of the first matters calling for the attention of a national foundation. In implementing plans for providing such training it should be possible to look for considerable help from university extra-mural departments and from the growing number of colleges of further education which have departments concerned with training for social work.

Finance

254   There are already some organizations which regard the training of volunteers as essential to their work, and recognize that the cost of training must form a substantial part of their expenditure. Their fund-raising activities take account of this,

whether they look to grants from public funds or elsewhere for their main sources of income. They appear, however, to be in a minority, and there are many voluntary bodies which fear that they would not have the means to develop programmes of training themselves, or to meet the cost of training for their volunteers. In our view, any organization which uses voluntary workers must recognize that their training, to whatever extent it may be required, should be a charge on the funds of the organization, and should make provision for it in estimating expenditure. Local authorities, too, should have regard to this important aspect of the work of voluntary bodies when considering applications from them for grants.

255   It has been argued, in this connection as in others, that people attach greater value to something for which they have to pay than to anything which is offered free; and that volunteers attending a course for which they are paying will be likely to attend more regularly, and to gain more from it, than they would if no charge were made. There may be some truth in this, but nevertheless we believe that what we have said in Chapter 6 about other expenses which may be incurred by voluntary workers can be applied also to the cost of training: we do not consider that volunteers themselves should be expected to meet the cost of whatever specific training they require for work in an agency which accepts their help. There is usually a charge for the general courses provided by educational bodies, and open to all, and normally those who attend these courses would expect to pay. If, however, a social service agency uses such a course as part of its training programme it may decide to pay the fees of its own volunteers or to reimburse them: this principle has already been adopted in relation to training provided for magistrates. Other training which is considered necessary for voluntary workers, whether it is provided on a co-operative basis for a number of agencies or by a particular organization for its own workers, should be free of charge to the volunteers.

Certificates

256   Any discussion of training tends to lead to the question

of whether those who have received it should thereby become eligible for some qualification, certificate or other form of recognition. At present certificates are awarded for knowledge or skill in areas where standards can be set and proficiency can be measured by examination or tests; for example, the certificates in first aid and home nursing of the British Red Cross Society, and the awards granted under the Duke of Edinburgh's Scheme. Such awards carry an assurance that a certain standard has been reached, and they provide those who hold them with a qualification which may be useful to them in seeking employment. In most of the fields in which voluntary workers are engaged, however, the award of certificates would be inappropriate. Much of the value of the work of volunteers lies in its personal character, and to attempt to standardize it might be to destroy it.

257   The purpose of training is always to enable the person who receives it to do better work and, where volunteers are concerned, this is its only purpose; though it may, as we have seen, bring other benefits. It does not, as in professional fields, have to serve as a guide for employers to appropriate gradings and salary scales; or as a measure of a person's fitness for membership of a professional body. Its results should be seen, but cannot readily be measured, and can rarely be standardized. We are aware that certificates of attendance are sometimes given to volunteers who have attended courses of training. These have some value as a record, and are often appreciated by the volunteers themselves; but it would be dangerous to regard such a certificate as any indication of the quality of a volunteer's work, or even of his knowledge.

Conclusions

258   We have surveyed in some detail the existing provisions for preparation and training, and have reached the conclusion that there are considerable needs which are not at present being met. We have suggested that everyone, and not only those who help in the social services, should have increased opportunities to learn about human needs and the services that exist

to meet them; and that educational bodies should provide these more comprehensively than they do at present. Although we regard such courses as education rather than training, agencies planning training schemes for volunteers may wish to use them as part of their plan. The nature of the specific preparation or training required by volunteers working for any agency must be worked out by the agency itself. It will certainly need the co-operation of educational bodies in carrying out its programme. It will normally fall to each organization using voluntary help to provide for its volunteers both initial briefing and such supervision as each of them may require.

259   The content of training and the methods to be used will depend upon the type of work to be done, but always, in some degree, the three elements of knowledge, skill and understanding will be required; and we have suggested how training might be planned to meet this requirement. We believe that the different users of voluntary help, with these principles in mind, will be able to find considerable areas of common ground in the training needed for their volunteers; and that the training required by all services should be reviewed and co-ordinated locally by a representative body set up for this purpose. Resources should be pooled and, wherever possible, training should be directed towards helping volunteers in some broad category of work, rather than towards the exclusive needs of a particular agency. We realize that the extension of training will have financial implications. We believe that many statutory and voluntary bodies do not yet recognize sufficiently that the cost of providing some training for volunteers is a necessary item of expenditure for any organization which uses their help, either directly or through the agency of other bodies. We hope that both government departments and local authorities will do all in their power to promote the extension of training facilities, both by encouragement and advice, and by financial support.

260   Finally, we suggest that a national foundation should be established, to be concerned not only with training, but with many aspects of voluntary work; and to provide a focus for the

local co-ordinating bodies. This suggestion will be developed and discussed in Chapter 10, in which we also have more to say about the financial implications of the suggestions which we have made.

Chapter 9

SOCIAL WORKERS AND VOLUNTEERS

261   We have already referred at several points in this report to difficulties and uncertainties which exist in relationships between social workers and volunteers, and to the need for clearer understanding, on both sides, of their respective functions, attributes, and outlook. We have given our reasons for believing that voluntary work has an essential place in the development of the social services; and we think that the vital role of professional social workers will be taken for granted by most readers. The need for social workers in the health and welfare services was argued in the report of the Working Party on Social Workers in the Local Authority Health and Welfare Services (the Younghusband Report), and accepted in the broadest possible sense by the Seebohm Committee. We do not propose to reiterate these arguments; we believe that the part which can and should be played by social workers in all the social services, not only as practitioners but also as initiators and advisers on policy, will not seriously be questioned.

Developments in Professional Social Work

262   It may be interesting to glance briefly at the way in which the social worker's role has developed over the last forty or fifty years. From 1920 onwards medical social work, and, later, probation and psychiatric social work, were developing professions in which training was seen to be necessary; and the London County Council was recruiting people with qualifications in social science as organizers of School Care Committee work. In other fields, social work was undertaken almost exclusively by voluntary organizations, with a small and slowly increasing number of workers with some basic training. The

second world war, and particularly the evacuation of children and family groups from London and other cities, brought local authorities in almost all parts of the country face to face with problems with which they had not previously had to contend. The help given by social workers, especially by psychiatric social workers and by some of the London School Care Committee organizers, whose services were made available in areas which received evacuees, was widely appreciated, and led a number of local authorities to appoint social workers to their own staffs. Most of the people then appointed were absorbed into the new or reorganized services brought into being by legislation in 1948. This legislation, and particularly, in the first instance, the Children Act, gave added stimulus to the demand by local authorities for social work staff; a demand which has been increasing ever since and which has never yet been satisfied. Meanwhile, Government Departments were recognizing the need for professional advisers on social work, both for themselves and for the local authorities for whose services they had some overall responsibility. The Ministry of Health appointed a Chief Welfare Officer in 1941, and since then social workers, both centrally and regionally, have come to play an influential part in the development and implementation of Government policy, both in the Department of Health and Social Security, and in the Home Office.

263   During the post-war years there have been further developments in the role of social workers and in what is expected of them. In local government they have taken their place, with members of other professions, in the ranks of chief officers and senior administrators; and have thus taken on new functions in administration and management. In the field, social workers are no longer regarded simply as sources of help to which members of other professions can turn in the interests of their clients. Their role has been extended to include diagnostic functions; they are expected to be sensitive not only to the problems of individuals and families, but increasingly of groups and communities, and to know how to call on the varied resources of the community for the alleviation of these problems. It is now taken for granted that practising social workers shall

be represented among the membership of advisory bodies and committees of enquiry concerned with social questions, whether local or national, to an extent which would not have been contemplated even twenty years ago.

Difficulties of Adjustment

264   It is not surprising that members of a profession whose boundaries have still to be defined, and which has grown up so rapidly and so recently, should still face some uncertainties; and that they should find it difficult to reconcile their view of themselves, as people trained to undertake skilled work and to deal with complex problems, with the idea that volunteers can help them in their work. The difficulty is particularly acute for those just completing their training; especially since they are likely to have found little or nothing in their training to help them to accept the idea, or to influence their attitude to voluntary help. Much of the training provided for social workers has been focused on ways of giving professional help to people with serious social or emotional difficulties. Newly trained workers will have become aware of the wide scope and complexity of the work, but are still uncertain of their own skills; and may, in spite of their training, find it difficult to see what their proper relationship with unqualified workers, whether paid or voluntary, should be. It is possible that they will never have met voluntary workers in action, and they may have a false idea of them as patronizing 'do-gooders' or as dangerous amateurs.

265   There are other factors which may lead both newly trained and experienced social workers to resist the idea of working with volunteers. They expect that their training and experience will enable them to help clients by means of a direct relationship; and find it difficult to believe that help which is given indirectly, through the co-operation of volunteers, will prove effective. The skill required for working with volunteers is different from, and additional to, that of direct personal work; and considerable readjustment may be needed from those who are asked to exercise it. There may, too, be certain regrets at the prospect of exchanging some of the interest and satisfaction of

personal relationships with clients for the different interest and satisfaction of seeing how a service can be improved and extended by the use of voluntary help and by greater community participation.

Implications for Training

266   We would certainly not wish to suggest that, in general, training bodies are unaware of all this. Many of them are now moving away from the emphasis on the problem of individuals and are directing more of their attention to seeing the client as a member of a group or community. Teaching about the structure and growth of communities, about the importance of enabling people to recognize and provide for their own needs, and about ways of doing this, has an increasingly important place in many courses. Students themselves are deeply concerned about social action, and the idea of community involvement finds a ready response. The concept of involving volunteers in the work done by social workers is, however, a further step which, in most courses, has not yet been taken. The changes and developments in the teaching of social work, to which we referred in paragraph 62, should, however, make it easier for both teachers and students to see that the relationship between a social worker and his client need not be an exclusive one, and to recognize the part which the community, and the volunteer as one of its representatives, can play. Understanding by social work students of the work of volunteers will be assisted by the fact that an increasing number of them have undertaken voluntary work of some kind before starting their training. There are also many students who undertake community service while at universities or colleges of further education. Social work students should be encouraged to see and know as much as possible of these activities and of those who take part in them.

267   It seems important to us that by the end of their training students should have some knowledge of what can be and is being done by voluntary workers in the many spheres which we have outlined, and some understanding of how their work relates to that of the professional. They should appreciate what

volunteers have to offer, not only in self-help and community activities but also in service of many other kinds, including their traditional role as pioneers. With this knowledge, and the attitude that it is possible and helpful for social workers and volunteers to work together as colleagues, they should be better prepared than many social workers are at present to accept and welcome voluntary help. Social work training may need to concentrate mainly on fostering desirable attitudes to voluntary work, leaving methods and techniques of using voluntary help to be developed through experience, assisted by short courses at a later stage. This would avoid some of the difficulties of adding yet another subject to courses which are already in danger of becoming overloaded; but its main advantage would be that social workers, as they gain experience of putting their own learning into practice, and confidence in themselves, are likely to become better able to see how their work can be complemented by that of volunteers. We have encouraging evidence of the way in which this is beginning to happen in some services. The Home Office, referring to the use of volunteers in probation and after-care, have quoted a Principal Probation Officer as saying: 'This recent experimental period has been most interesting, indeed exciting, and has demonstrated that we have a new tool which, used properly, will aid and improve our efforts in this particular field.'

268   Field work, which provides observation and supervised experience of co-operation between social workers and volunteers, can form an important and valuable part of training. The Council for Training in Social Work, in their evidence to us, emphasized this, and suggested that more attention could well be given by tutors and field-work teachers, at their regular meetings, to ways of giving students greater opportunities for seeing and learning about the contribution which voluntary workers can make. These meetings would also provide opportunities for discussion of what students should be learning to expect from volunteers. Students themselves might be encouraged to think about kinds of work which could appropriately be undertaken by volunteers; and about ways in which their use might be extended in services with which the students are becoming

familiar, and what this implies for their own role as professional social workers.

269   The Report of the Study Group on Training for Community Work, *Community Work and Social Change*, devotes a chapter (Chapter 11) to the field-work training both of people who are proposing to take up full-time community work, and of other social work students. It refers to the selection of agencies for field training, which, it says:

'. . . would depend on the standard of work of the agency, the opportunities it is able to offer for practice and learning relevant to the purpose of the course, the agency's interest in student training, and ability to offer such necessary facilities as skilled staff, time, space, etc.; common aims in the approach and methods of the agency, and of the course, and the possibility of developing close working relationships.'

The report goes on to list the qualities and responsibilities required of field-work teachers or supervisors, and to refer to the present shortage of people of the capacity required. Those responsible for the training of social workers are very familiar with the problem of finding enough field-work placements of the desired standard for their students. Our evidence suggests that, as might have been expected, this difficulty is even greater in the field of community work than in the case work services with their longer tradition of professional social work. However, we understand the Joint University Council for Social and Public Administration are taking steps to improve this situation.

270   If training bodies are to give more attention to preparing their students for working with volunteers they will need to be able to place them, for part of their training, in services where voluntary workers are playing a significant part. Such placements are scarce at present, and it is important that all services which can offer students the opportunity of working with volunteers, together with the other necessary facilities for field-work training, should do so to the utmost of their ability. There is also at present a noticeable lack of case material which

illustrates the work of volunteers in a constructive way, and every opportunity should be taken to make good this shortage. We would suggest that further consideration might usefully be given by the Advisory Council for Probation and After-Care, the Central Training Council in Child Care, and the Council for Training in Social Work to the question of how social workers can learn to make fuller use of voluntary help.

271   Students will need to learn that volunteers work at many different levels and to be guided between assuming, on the one hand, that only the simplest tasks are appropriate for them and, on the other, that all are capable of skilled supportive work. In their field-work, students should be given opportunities of seeing as many different types and levels of voluntary work as possible, but the time which can be devoted to this will inevitably be limited. It is usually not difficult to arrange for students to see volunteers engaged in practical tasks, and they can certainly gain from this experience; but it may be better to concentrate on showing them the less obvious contribution of volunteers, and the quality of the relationship which can exist between a voluntary worker and his clients. For example, the organization of a meals-on-wheels service is important and the distribution of meals provides interesting opportunities for meeting a number of different clients, but it cannot show much about continuing relationships. A student might gain much more real understanding of what voluntary work is by accompanying a volunteer, who has time to be unhurried, on one visit to an old person by whom the volunteer has come to be regarded as an old and trusted friend. Students in the medical social work departments of hospitals should have opportunities of meeting voluntary workers and seeing what they can offer the patients, not only by way of practical help, but also by being people 'from outside' who have time to talk and even to gossip. In services where volunteers are already being used to complement the work of social workers, students may begin to understand their respective functions and see how, when they are combined, a new dimension can be brought to the work: with the result that the social worker and volunteer together can offer something which is more than the sum of their separate efforts.

175

272   The Joint University Council for Social and Public Administration referred, in evidence to us, to the importance of the impressions gained by students in their field-work, and to the use which can be made of these impressions in theoretical teaching. They say:

'It is probably when undertaking field work in an agency in which voluntary workers are part of the structure, that students first begin to think about the role of volunteers, the quality of their work and their integration within the agency. Above all, the attitude of the staff towards them will influence the students' ideas and they may return to the University full of admiration or severely critical. In either case the University tutor has opportunity in individual discussion to consider why the arrangement was satisfactory or the reverse, and stimulate thinking about the positive contribution of volunteers.'

If some of our suggestions regarding the extended use and better organization of voluntary help, and improved provisions for the preparation and training of volunteers, are put into effect, more agencies should eventually become able to undertake this part of the training of social workers. One essential is that organizations using voluntary workers should be clearer than some of them are at present about the respective functions of social workers, other paid staff, and volunteers, and the types of work appropriate for each category in their particular settings.

The Need of Voluntary Organizations for a Balanced Team

273   In Chapter 5 we indicated certain fields in which we considered that more use might be made of voluntary help. These included statutory services which have not yet fully developed the use of volunteers, and some voluntary services which have become over-professionalized. There are also some movements in which the reverse is true and where there is little or no recognition of the need for social workers. When new projects are initiated by volunteers there may be among these volunteers some who are themselves social workers. Whether or not this is the case it is not unusual for such projects to bring in social workers after a time, when the need for a core of pro-

fessional staff becomes apparent. In the past, some agencies have gone so far as almost to have ceased to use volunteers at all. Some, on the other hand, do not recognize that there is any need to involve social workers in what they are undertaking. They may not accept that there is an essential part to be played by professional workers, or they may have come to regard their volunteers as near-professionals.

274   An example of the latter type of service is that of Marriage Guidance Councils. We have already described the careful selection procedure, and have referred to the importance which is attached both to this and to the training of voluntary counsellors. The quality of their training is admirable, but it rarely extends beyond four concentrated weekends of study; and cannot be expected to qualify those who receive it for work which requires professional knowledge and skill. Local Marriage Guidance Councils make use of consultants from psychiatry and other professions; but not only employ no social workers in their own service, but have, in many places, very limited contact with those in other services. This may be to some extent the result of their own high standards and the emphasis placed in the training of counsellors on the need to maintain the strictest confidence regarding their clients' affairs. It does not, however, take account of the fact that social workers have similar standards, and in some fields are undertaking very similar work. We believe that increased co-operation between Marriage Guidance Councils and social workers would enable the Councils to give a better service to their clients than they do at present. We hope that there may be a move towards a greater use of social workers in this service, particularly for the selection and allocation of cases; and to provide consultation and guidance for the carefully selected, appropriately trained, and often gifted volunteers.

Respective Functions of Social Workers and Volunteers

275   We believe that as the roles of social workers and volunteers continue to evolve there will be changes in the view of what work requires to be done by a social worker and what is appro-

priate to a volunteer. In any particular situation the functions of social workers and volunteers need to be defined, but in general the boundary must remain flexible. There are, however, many kinds of work which can be seen clearly to fall on one side or the other. On the volunteers' side, as we have seen, much valuable work is done which would not in any case be undertaken by social workers. If there were no volunteers, paid labour might be employed for some of this work, but much of it would not be done at all. We refer to services such as house decorating and gardening for old people; playing with or reading to children in hospitals; provision of transport; much of the work done by some of the Good Neighbour schemes; and many other tasks for which specially acquired skill or knowledge is not required. Some types of work which certainly do call for special knowledge or skill also come into this category, for example, those information services whose function is not to offer advice on personal problems but, when necessary, to indicate where it may be obtained; and to provide information on many other subjects. Services of all these kinds, when properly organized, can be valuable adjuncts to social work, but it is not necessary to have social workers either to organize, to supervise or to intervene in them.

276   It is also possible to distinguish some functions which are proper to social workers and should be undertaken by them. Their training is designed to enable them to consider the causes and likely repercussions of a problem and not merely its symptoms; to help a client to assess his needs, and to plan ways in which he can be helped. This involves gaining his co-operation and enabling him to feel that he is being helped, even though what he may need is far removed from what he originally asked for. These functions of assessment and planning, in dealing with people's problems, usually fall outside the role of volunteers, though voluntary help can be utilized at many stages in carrying out a plan. The social worker has a continuing supportive and interpretative role in relation to volunteers, and acts as an 'enabler' and mobilizer of other resources. He may, too, have to make vital decisions which can affect the life of a client and of those about him. Among other types of work

178

which need to be undertaken by social workers are certain statutory duties of probation officers, mental welfare officers, child care officers and others, which cannot legally be delegated to volunteers. There are also duties, such as that of visiting boarded-out children which, apart from the fact that they call for a high degree of skill and knowledge, are so responsible, and the consequences of misjudgment or negligence may be so serious, that most officials would consider that they ought not to ask volunteers to undertake them.

277   We asked professional associations of social workers for their views as to the respective functions of social workers and volunteers. Some of the opinions expressed referred to the questions of accountability and responsibility for statutory duties which are mentioned above. Some spoke of the danger of giving responsible work, requiring a degree of skill, to volunteers who were insufficiently prepared or trained for it, and emphasized the need for training rather than any inherent objection to using voluntary help. Others, such as the two quoted below, indicated what some social workers saw as the limitations of voluntary work:

(a) 'The professional is trained and equipped to work at depths and with complexities beyond the range of the voluntary worker and is essentially concerned with long-term goals. These goals may be uncertain and changing, and there is always the possibility of having to take emergency decisions. The professional has an interpretative, supportive and rehabilitative role, with concern and help for other members of the client's family. The voluntary worker can only be expected to deal with particular situations, as they separately arise, in a practical manner, and often through the medium of friendly contact.'

(b) 'It is considered that voluntary workers should not be involved in situations where the focus of treatment is an emotional problem concerning family relationships and the client might involve the voluntary worker to manipulate the situation. . . . The voluntary worker is not expected to become involved in the motivation or behaviour problems of a patient, and may need professional help to limit the demands and pressures of clients.'

278   It appears to us that these opinions express too cautious a view, and that with the development of training and supervision for voluntary workers a partnership of a more positive and constructive kind should be possible between social workers and volunteers. Provided that each has learned what the other can do, what is the purpose and effect of the social worker's training, and how it can be complemented by the volunteer's freedom of approach and ability to give time to individuals, their combined efforts can be more effective, in the interests of their clients, than either could alone. The way in which their work is divided will depend on the social worker's attitude and his ability to see the possibilities of voluntary work; and also, of course, on the quality of the voluntary help at his disposal, and the availability at a given time of a volunteer able to meet the needs of a particular client. Some social workers can work through volunteers in providing a supportive service to an extent that might not be possible for others; nor would this degree of delegation necessarily be appropriate everywhere. There is room for great variety and flexibility in the patterns of co-operation, and it is important that boundaries should not become fixed or rigid.

279   In general, then, we believe that in any personal service which is concerned with social problems, whether it is provided by a statutory or a voluntary agency, there is a need for social workers and a place for volunteers. Although they are equipped for their work in very different ways, there are some areas in which it is not possible to draw precise boundaries between the functions appropriate to either type of worker; though it is always necessary for each to be aware of what the other is doing in relation to a particular client. This is not to say that they are identical or interchangeable; and even when they are doing similar kinds of work there are likely to be considerable differences in their ways of doing them. Their services are complementary, and there is still much to be learned about how to make the most effective use of their combined resources. It must

also be remembered that the effectiveness of any service depends to a considerable extent on its acceptability to clients, and there may be a need to learn more about the feelings of clients of different kinds and in different circumstances towards being offered help by either professional people or voluntary workers.

Chapter 10

IMPLICATIONS FOR ACTION

280   In this chapter we bring together and consider the main implications of our study, particularly as these suggest lines of action. Many people recognize that a 'new look' is urgently needed. A few agencies are already well ahead in promoting some developments of the kind we advocate. Nevertheless, we offer our findings, some of which may seem of a common sense rather than a revolutionary nature, as a basis for review and action. A summary of our specific conclusions and recommendations is given at the end of this chapter.

The Place of Voluntary Help

281   As our work has proceeded we have become increasingly convinced of the special quality and value of the volunteer's contribution. We see him as essential to any significant extention in the range and impact of the social services. As a pioneer he will continue, as in the past, to make his special impact. His place in established social services needs to be made more explicit and ways must be found of ensuring that he is used more effectively.

282   We have been struck by the need for both statutory and voluntary bodies to formulate more clearly their aims and policies regarding the use of volunteers. This would be to the advantage of both the agencies and the volunteers themselves. Vagueness about why volunteers are needed and how they fit into a total structure is at the root of many current problems of recruitment and deployment. We do not wish to imply that the functions of volunteers can be determined by any precise formula, or that they should be the same in all services. On the contrary, we believe it important to preserve great flexibility, an

open mind, and readiness to keep constantly under review the use which is and can be made of voluntary help. However, every agency should have a general policy regarding the kinds of work to be carried out by volunteers, the ways in which their help is to be obtained and organized, and, perhaps most important of all, a clear idea of their relationship with professional and other staff. The consideration of other important questions, such as the number of voluntary workers which, at any time, a particular service needs and can use, the kinds of preparation or training which they will require, and how these are to be provided, must then follow.

283   Voluntary workers have a unique contribution to make, and should not be regarded, in established services, as a substitute for professional staff. Nor should they be used, in ordinary circumstances, to do work for which in the service concerned it is accepted practice to employ paid staff. The object of making greater use of voluntary help should always be to extend and improve a service, by adding something to what is already being done, or by opening up new possibilities.

284   It is unlikely that all professional staff in the social services, social workers and others, will be immediately convinced of the value of voluntary work. Social workers are, however, becoming perceptibly more receptive to the idea of working with volunteers than they have been, generally speaking, in the past. We hope that further developments in the training of social workers will help them to understand better the contribution which voluntary workers can make, as well as their own role in relation to it, and to welcome it more warmly. Social workers are often in a key position to demonstrate this contribution to members of other professions, who may be sceptical or even antagonistic. There remains much to be done in the education of professional opinion, both by social workers themselves and by others who are concerned with the organization of voluntary work. We greatly welcome the recent appointment by King Edward's Hospital Fund of a social worker to further the use and appreciation of voluntary workers in the health services.

Administrative and Financial Considerations

285   We are not concerned in this report with the organization of voluntary bodies except in so far as it affects the work of
volunteers; but since the quality of management and the way in
which services are administered, whether by statutory or voluntary agencies, have a direct bearing on this, we cannot ignore the
significance of some administrative aspects. These include the
employment of appropriately qualified staff, clarification of the
functions of voluntary, paid, and professional workers, provision of information at all levels, and arrangements for the
preparation or training of volunteers. Voluntary organizations
which attach due importance to such matters are obliged to set
up an effective administrative structure and to ensure its
continuity.

286   Government departments and local authorities on the
whole subscribe to the idea that voluntary work is necessary if
the scope of the personal social services is to be extended and its
quality enriched. But hitherto, with some notable exceptions,
the tendency has been to ignore, or to give a wholly inadequate
response to, requests for financial support to voluntary bodies
for administrative purposes. Some of these bodies have highly
competent, gifted and devoted voluntary workers who have
been prepared, over the years, to undertake the work of administration; but such an arrangement can no longer be regarded as a long-term solution to the problem of organization.
Voluntary bodies are likely to have to pay for administrative
staff, and it is useless to suppose that competent people can be
recruited indefinitely at salaries far below the normal rate.
Without sufficient financial support, however this is provided,
desirable standards of organization and performance cannot
be achieved.

287   Certain voluntary organizations can be taken as examples of the way in which adequate financial resources, whether
derived from public or from voluntary funds, make it possible
to provide a particularly effective administrative structure. The
British Red Cross Society, which commands large resources,

has an impressive organization, and is able to pay constant attention to providing and improving training for its volunteers, both centrally and locally. The Women's Royal Voluntary Service through grants from public funds has been able to maintain both a Headquarters administration and a regional and local organization. This has ensured its ability to respond to needs of many kinds. The National Marriage Guidance Council, with a substantial Home Office grant, and financial support from authorities to its local Councils, has a strong Headquarters administration, high standards of selection and training, informative publications, and wide national coverage.

288   Some other voluntary bodies, both national and local, are far less well placed. Direct support from central government funds at national level and grants from local authorities to local bodies are rarely adequate to meet administrative requirements, though again there are some honourable exceptions. Voluntary support is far harder to obtain for administrative purposes than for work which can be seen to be of direct benefit to those in need. People are not only reluctant to contribute towards administrative expenses, but there is a noticeable tendency to criticize any voluntary body rash enough to suggest that it needs money for such things as staff salaries, buildings which are reasonably comfortable to work in, conveniently equipped and attractive to the public, and other expenses involved in organization. Good organization is essential for any service. An increased use of volunteers, their recruitment, selection, preparation and training, intelligent deployment and guidance necessarily presuppose an administrative structure that costs money. Without this, effort will be wasted and inefficiency is inescapable.

289   Hitherto many voluntary bodies have been able to establish themselves and make progress, thanks to the help and encouragement received from charitable Trusts. These Trusts have shown courage and imagination, in that they have been prepared to underwrite pioneering efforts, often of a kind that could not be expected to command immediate official support. This process continues and is one for which the public, as well as

the bodies receiving help, should be profoundly grateful. We believe, however, that there is a pattern of development that should normally apply: and that after the initial stage of pioneering and demonstration, provided that the scheme is judged to be of value to the community, it should be possible to expect that some financial responsibility will be assumed at the appropriate Government level. No doubt in the development of new plans and projects relating to volunteers the help of Trusts will continue to be invoked. Nevertheless, we think that this is primarily a field that justifies support from public funds, since central Departments or local authorities, as the case may be, stand to gain immeasurably from resources used in this way.

290   Thus we should like to see stronger backing from central Government departments for the extended use of voluntary help in all the statutory social services. In some spheres a good deal of encouragement has already been given, particularly in probation and after-care, the Youth Service and in hospitals; in some others there has so far been little or no clear expression of policy. It is not enough simply to advocate more use of voluntary help, or to offer advice on ways in which it might be turned to good advantage. The expectation is that by drawing as fully as possible on all that volunteers are prepared to give, better services would be offered than those provided by paid staff alone. This would involve considerably less cost than if a comparable improvement were attempted by the employment of much larger paid staffs. But it cannot be done at no cost at all, and we hope that such action will be taken at Government level as will ensure that the necessary resources are made available directly or through local authorities. We also hope that the advisory staff of Government Departments and their inspectors will take steps to become fully informed about the use of volunteers in the services with which they are concerned, and will encourage and help its development.

Local Authorities and Voluntary Workers

291   We have referred at a number of points in this report to the question of how voluntary help for local authority services

can best be obtained and organized. We ourselves started from the point of view that an extended use of volunteers in these services would necessitate a very considerable increase in recruitment, training and allocation by voluntary organizations, rather than the development of the direct recruitment of volunteers by local authorities. There have been some changes in our views as our work has proceeded, and we believe these to be in line with changing opinions generally among local authorities and other statutory and voluntary agencies which recruit and use voluntary help. We are convinced that whether or not local authority social services are in the fairly near future made the responsibility of a combined social work department, they will provide scope for a very much wider use of voluntary help than is to be seen at present. We do not, however, think that local authorities should confine themselves to any one method of obtaining this help. We believe that a combination of methods, used according to circumstances and the kind of work to be done, will prove the best solution.

292   We expect to see a continuing increase in the number of voluntary bodies which not only recruit volunteers but also employ qualified staff and can offer a reliable standard of service. Such bodies could be used with confidence to undertake specific projects on behalf of local authorities, thus acting as an extension of the local authorities' own personal services. They could provide a valuable additional resource and might greatly increase the possibility of maintaining long-term contacts with clients who at present lack any continuing link with the social services. Volunteers engaged in this work would, in addition, be able to ensure that the attention of the statutory services was drawn to clients with further needs. In services where professional workers are not directly involved there may also be great advantages in leaving the selection, organization and supervision of volunteers to an appropriate voluntary agency. The preparation and allocation of volunteers, the organization of teams where necessary, and the filling of gaps, the personal interest and encouragement to which volunteers are entitled, and the sorting out of their own problems, all require consider-

able expenditure of time and effort. Local authorities may be glad to leave some or all of this work to voluntary bodies, and should be prepared to make adequate payment, by way of grants to these bodies, for the service which they receive.

293   It is probable, however, that the largest increase in the use of voluntary help by local authorities will be in those activities in which volunteers complement the work of the authorities' own social workers. For such work, authorities are likely to prefer that volunteers shall be directly accountable to them. Social workers who expect to have volunteers working closely with them will usually wish to have a say in the selection of the volunteers, and the allocation of work to them; and to ensure that they receive the preparation, training and supervision which they need. For these reasons we believe that the recruitment, selection and training of voluntary workers by local authorities is likely to increase. Many have at present little experience in these directions, and will need to develop methods of recruiting and selecting volunteers, and of organizing their work.

Organizers of Voluntary Work

294   We have described the important part which the organizer of voluntary work has to play in both statutory and voluntary services. As our enquiries proceeded we became increasingly aware of the significance of the organizer's function, which was perhaps most clearly conveyed to us by volunteers themselves. It was not that they asked in so many words to be better organized, or that all were conscious of the need to the same degree. Some were working in services with an effective organization and concern for individual volunteers; and this tended to be reflected in their identification with the agency for which they worked, their realization that they were part of a movement and not isolated units, and often resulted in greater confidence in themselves and satisfaction in their work. Others, however, revealed feelings of isolation, of lack of communication with their headquarters, or of difficulty in knowing where to turn for advice. Some felt that no one was really interested in what they were doing, that they were forgotten or overlooked,

or that the work which they had been asked to do was either too difficult or too simple. The fact that in spite of this they continued to offer voluntary service says much for their good will, but does not make it any less necessary to provide better arrangements for them.

295   Every agency which uses voluntary help, whether it recruits its own volunteers, relies on the services of members of voluntary organizations, or employs a combination of both methods, needs some person to undertake the organizing functions which we describe earlier. According to the type of service, the number of volunteers, and other circumstances, the organizer may be engaged full-time or part-time on this work; and may be a social worker, a member of staff with some other qualification, or an experienced volunteer. In some settings, particularly those where the primary purpose is not that of providing a social work service, as for example in hospitals and prisons, the task of helping members of other professions to understand and appreciate the voluntary contribution may be a particularly important one for the organizer. At present no specific training is available for organizers of voluntary work. We have suggested that short courses should be provided, and have mentioned some of the subjects which such courses might cover.

Volunteer Bureaux

296   We have been impressed by the value of volunteer bureaux in the comparatively few places where they are to be found at present; and we believe that there is a need and a demand for a network of such centres to cover the whole country. They can provide information about opportunities for voluntary service to people who are interested, but who without some preliminary advice and discussion might never make a direct approach to any particular agency; or might become frustrated and discouraged because they cannot obtain comprehensive information about local needs for voluntary help. The bureaux can thus be of service both to prospective volunteers and to agencies needing voluntary help. They may also undertake

active recruiting, either for particular jobs of which they have been notified by the agencies concerned, or for people prepared to offer help in quite a general way and willing to be put in touch with services which need them. Through their work, bureaux acquire considerable knowledge of what voluntary workers have to offer, and may thus be in a position to give helpful advice to agencies which are considering how to extend their use of volunteers.

297   Existing bureaux are financed partly from voluntary sources or Trusts, and partly by grants from local authorities. They cannot be maintained without financial support, and we believe that local authorities should bear the major responsibility for their finance in the future.

Recruitment

298   We have found some support for what we believe to be the fairly general view that voluntary work is a mainly middle-class activity, though the predominance is by no means over-whelming. This situation may be due, at least in part, to the practice adopted by many organizations of relying on personal introductions as their major means of obtaining new workers; a practice which tends to perpetuate recruitment from one particular type of background. We are convinced that people who are willing to help others, and have the necessary qualities of understanding and sensitiveness, are to be found in all sections of society. Some environments provide more opportunities than others for giving informal help to friends and neighbours, and therefore perhaps less incentive to offering service elsewhere; but we believe that there are great resources which have not yet been tapped, and that the fields from which volunteers are drawn might be enormously widened if active and well-thought-out recruiting efforts were brought into use. We have already referred to the need for social service agencies to define more clearly their reasons for seeking voluntary workers, and what they expect of them; and to the effect which this might have in facilitating recruitment. There is also a need for study and experiment in new methods of reaching potential volunteers. In particular we

believe that considerably more older people, including those recently retired from full-time work, might be drawn into the ranks of voluntary workers if it were made known that there are specific jobs to be done in which their maturity and experience could be fully used. With the development of more active recruiting efforts, and a clearer formulation of the purposes for which volunteers are required, and their place in the general scheme, selection too, will acquire increasing importance. Methods of selection need to be further developed and more widely used.

Preparation and Training

299   We consider that all volunteers need some degree of preparation for their work, though the form which it takes, the methods used, and the time which needs to be devoted to it, will vary almost as widely as do the kinds of work which volunteers undertake. We hope to see an extension of general education about the social services, and for this we look to the educational bodies, radio and television. Specific training for voluntary work in the social services needs to be adapted to the requirements of people who, for the most part, do not regard themselves as students. It should be made easy for them to understand the purpose of their training, and to see a close connection between what is being taught and the actual work which they are expecting to do. Informal group teaching is preferable to formal lecturing. Imaginative methods, and especially those which involve the students as much as possible, should be used.

Local Joint Committees

300   Greater co-operation at local level between all statutory and voluntary agencies using the services of voluntary workers would be an important step towards the extension of training facilities. The pooling of resources, and the provision whenever possible of training which will meet the needs of volunteers working for a number of different agencies, should lead to economy of effort and help to minimize expense. To this end we have suggested the setting up of local Joint Committees.

Such Committees, which should be representative of all local interests, would also prove a valuable forum for the discussion of other aspects of the work of volunteers in relation to the needs of the local community and its services.

A National Foundation

301   In Chapter 8 we referred briefly to the need for the establishment of a national body, which could co-ordinate the activities of the local Joint Committees, and serve as a focus for all aspects of the work of volunteers in the social services. We attach great importance to the setting up of such a body which would be concerned with volunteers of all ages which we should like to call the Volunteer Foundation. We believe that organizations which are associated with volunteers in any way would be likely to make use of the Foundation, and that they should be encouraged to become subscribing members. The Foundation would require a small staff, able, through their qualifications or experience, to communicate easily with volunteers, social workers and administrators, to assemble information, promote studies and pilot projects, advise on training schemes and methods; and generally encourage a positive attitude to the whole field of voluntary work. Without such a body we think it unlikely that the necessary impetus and guidance will be available to achieve what we regard as urgently needed developments.

302   We consider that the Volunteer Foundation should be of independent status; but we do not propose to make detailed suggestions here regarding its constitution. We considered carefully whether there was any existing body which could reasonably be expected to add responsibilities of the kind envisaged to its present functions, and came to the conclusion that there was not. The National Council of Social Service is not sufficiently identified with studies, training, or professional groups: the National Institute for Social Work Training is too much centred on training to undertake so broad a role: and the Social Work Advisory Service is exclusively concerned with questions relating to careers and training for professional social work. The

Advisory Council for Probation and Aftercare, the Central Training Council in Child Care, and the Council for Training in Social Work seemed equally inappropriate. We should like to think, however, that all these bodies would be closely associated with the Volunteer Foundation and give it all possible co-operation and support. We hope that our sponsors, in consultation with the Government Departments concerned, and with local authority interests, would do whatever is practicable to get the Foundation established with all possible speed.

303   With regard to finance, we should hope that the Government would look favourably on the Volunteer Foundation as a subject for a generous initial grant from public funds. During this initial period, methods by which continuing financial support might be obtained could be worked out. Such a Foundation would clearly be a strong candidate for some support from voluntary sources; but it takes time to establish the necessary financial structure. We should hope that, in any case, some continuing grant from public funds would be available. To put it at its lowest, statutory support for an organization which will greatly increase the potentialities of the social services is a very worthwhile investment.

Conclusion

304   It may be trite to say that the social services are at a transitional stage. We await Government action on the See-bohm Report. The Report of the Royal Commission on Local Government is likely to suggest radical changes in local government structure. The future pattern of the health service is uncertain. All these changing situations in the field of Government must have their repercussions on voluntary organizations which, in their turn, further affect our sphere of interest. This state of flux and uncertainty is evident in other spheres, in education, in the growing influence of mass media and in early attempts to make a reality of community work.

305   We see at least one common conviction, namely that the gap between social needs and social provision must be narrowed.

N   193

Wherever we look this gap can be detected. It cannot be completely filled simply by the deployment of more workers but, in so far as personal service of some kind is involved, the resources which voluntary workers represent could prove a major factor. It is for this reason that we have no hesitation in presenting a case for the devotion of substantial funds from statutory resources to enable our proposals to be put into effect.

CONCLUSIONS AND RECOMMENDATIONS

(Numbers in parentheses refer to paragraphs in the text of the report)

THE ROLE OF THE VOLUNTARY WORKER

1. *The place of volunteers in the expanding social services.* Voluntary workers have an essential part to play in the provision of personal social services. The special contribution of volunteers, as representing community participation in the social services, and as complementing the work of paid staff, should be recognized. (117, 118, 123, 124, 281)
2. *Clarification of aims.* The place of voluntary workers in each service or area of need should be re-examined, in order that their roles may be clarified and greater purpose and direction given to their work. (125, 282)
3. *Review of tasks appropriate for voluntary workers.* The distinction between practical tasks appropriate for volunteers, and those for which paid staff are employed, should be kept under review. Except in an emergency, volunteers should not be used, in public services, to undertake manual or domestic tasks, for which paid workers are normally employed. (119, 120, 121, 283)

ORGANIZATION OF THE WORK OF VOLUNTEERS

4. *Organizers of voluntary service.* There should be a full-time or part-time organizer of the work of volunteers in every service in which they are employed: the post may be held by a paid or voluntary worker without professional qualifications; or in certain circumstances by a social worker. (127, 145, 146, 294, 295)
5. *Organization by statutory and voluntary bodies.* Voluntary bodies have important continuing functions in obtaining and organizing the help of volunteers, and we expect that

195

these functions will also increasingly be exercised by statutory bodies. Agencies of both kinds must ensure that there is an effective organization with adequate financial support. (128, 132–134, 285–293)

6. *Volunteer bureaux.* There should be a comprehensive network of volunteer bureaux, as centres of advice and information for volunteers and to assist statutory and voluntary bodies which need their help. Their functions would include recruitment and preliminary selection and the keeping of records of volunteers. (143, 163, 164, 179, 180, 296)

7. *Financing of bureaux.* Local authorities should bear the major responsibility for financing volunteer bureaux. (143, 297)

8. *The volunteers' need for membership of an organization.* Volunteers who are not members of an organization which gives them a sense of corporate identity may wish to establish an organization of their own, and should be encouraged to do so. (151)

9. *Expenses of volunteers.* Statutory and voluntary agencies should expect to pay travelling and other out-of-pocket expenses of their voluntary workers. (155)

10. *Insurance.* The insurance of voluntary workers should be considered by every organization which uses them, and every volunteer should know what arrangements are made. (156)

11. *Identification.* Each voluntary worker should be provided with some authorization or other evidence of his identity and bona fides. (157)

RECRUITMENT AND SELECTION

12. *Extension of recruitment.* Active recruiting methods should be developed with a view to increasing the number of volunteers and widening the fields from which they are drawn. (165, 166, 298)

13. *Organization of recruitment.* In every agency using volunteers there should be some person responsible for the organization of recruitment. (171)

14. *Criteria for recruitment.* Agencies should formulate their requirements more precisely and specify more clearly what

kinds of people are wanted for particular services or specific jobs. (167)

15. *Recruitment of older people.* Particular attention should be paid to the recruitment of older people and to ways of attracting the recently retired to work which is specially appropriate for them. (169, 170)

16. *Selection.* Every agency which needs to select volunteers should develop selection procedures applicable to their fields of work, and apply them. (183)

PREPARATION AND TRAINING

17. *Preparation.* All volunteers need preparation for their work. (186, 187)

18. *General educational courses.* Courses on the social services should be provided more generally by educational bodies in order that people of all ages may be aware of social needs and services. (210)

19. *Mass media.* Radio and television have an important part to play in developing interest in voluntary service and disseminating information about it. (217)

20. *Schools.* Voluntary service by school children is to be encouraged, but participation in community service should not be made part of the curriculum and undertaken as a school subject. (211–214)

21. *Organization of training.* In each agency there should be a person who is responsible for the promotion of training for its voluntary workers, and for ensuring that they are able to obtain it. (251, 252)

22. *Content of training.* The content of training should be closely related to the volunteer's needs and the work which he will do. (218–226)

23. *Methods.* Methods of training should be informal and flexible to suit the needs of people of a wide age range, from varied backgrounds, and often not academically inclined. (227)

24. *Supervision.* Supervision, consultation and advice should always be available to volunteers, and are particularly important for those whose work involves close personal relationships with clients. (233–237)

25. *Further training.* Short courses, conferences, seminars and discussion groups should be available to volunteers who have had some training and have started work. (242)

26. *Training for special responsibilities.* Short courses should be provided for both paid and voluntary workers who undertake work as organizers, trainers or supervisors of volunteers. (159, 243)

27. *Local Joint Committees.* Training should be co-ordinated locally, resources pooled, and courses planned to meet the common needs of volunteers in a number of different services. To assist in co-ordination, and to provide a local focus for the discussion and provision of training, Joint Committees should be established. (248, 249, 300)

28. *Financing training.* Statutory and voluntary agencies should regard the cost of training for volunteers as an essential item of expenditure and make provision for it: local authorities should take account of this in considering their grants to voluntary bodies. (254, 255)

SOCIAL WORKERS AND VOLUNTEERS

30. *The training of social workers.* Greater attention should be paid in both the theoretical and the field training of social workers, to increasing their understanding of the contribution of voluntary workers, both as individuals and as demonstrating the growing participation by the community in the provision of social services. (266–272, 284)

31. *Functions of social workers and volunteers.* In all the social services there is a place for volunteers, but they should not be expected to undertake work for which professional training is required. Agencies which undertake to help people with serious social or personal problems need professional staff as well as voluntary workers. (278, 279)

A NATIONAL BODY

32. *The Volunteer Foundation.* We recommend the setting up of a national body financed initially from public funds; to be called the Volunteer Foundation and be a focus for all aspects of the work of volunteers. (250, 301, 302)

APPENDIX I

List of Organizations and Individuals who Assisted the Committee

The symbol * indicates that the organization replied to the relevant questionnaire, which in many instances involved submitting replies from a number of local branches (see Appendix II). Representatives of many of these organizations, including voluntary workers, gave oral evidence to the Committee, either formally or informally. Many welcomed our members to their centres or to training courses.

In addition to those individuals mentioned there were many others who gave the Committee valuable help, some of whom preferred not to be identified publicly.

* Albany Institute
* Alcoholics Anonymous
* Apex Charitable Trust
* Army Cadet Force Association
* Association of Child Care Officers
* Association of Children's Officers
* Association of Directors of Welfare Services
* Association of Family Caseworkers
* Association of Psychiatric Social Workers
* Association of Social Workers
* Bath Link of Friendship
* Beaconsfield Advisory Centre and Good Neighbour Service
* Bede House Association
  Benenden Voluntary Service
  Bentley, Rev. James, Secretary, Stretfield Council of Churches
* Bernhard Baron St George's Jewish Settlement
  Birkenhead Probation and Aftercare Department
  Birmingham Council of Social Service
* Birmingham Settlement
* Bishop Creighton House, Fulham

Blackfriars Family Counsellors Project
* Bournville Council of Churches Social Responsibility Project
* Boys' Brigade
Brent Council of Social Service
* British Association of Residential Settlements
British Broadcasting Corporation
* British Epilepsy Association
* British Red Cross Society
* Cambridge House University Settlement
Cambridge University Social Service Organization
* Camden Council of Social Service
* The Cameron Group
* Camphill Village Trust
* Catholic Marriage Advisory Council
* Central Churches Group
* Central Council for the Disabled
* Christ Church and Methodist Chelsea Good Neighbour Scheme
* Circle Trust, Ipswich
Collett, Mr. David, Secretary, Blackfriars Settlement Federation
Collins, Miss Patricia. Tutor, Certificate in Social Work Course—North Western Polytechnic
* Community Service Volunteers
Community Transport
* Conference of Principal Probation Officers
Council for Training in Social Work
* County Welfare Officers' Society
Coventry City Probation and Aftercare Department
Department of Education and Science
Dickson, C.B.E., Mr Alec, Director, Community Service Volunteers
Disablement Income Group
Exeter Council of Social Service
Eyden, Miss J., Senior Lecturer in Social Administration, University of Nottingham
Family Planning Association
* Family Service Units
* Family Welfare Association

Finzi, Miss J., Voluntary Help Organizer, St Thomas's Hospital

* Fish Scheme, Bexley
* Fish Scheme, Oxford

Fleet, Mr D. M., Chief Welfare Officer, London Borough of Hounslow

* Girl Guides Association

Groombridge, M.A., Mr Brian, formerly Deputy Secretary, National Institute of Adult Education (England and Wales) now Education Officer, Independent Television Authority

Hanna, Mrs S., Organizer of Volunteers, St Christopher's Hospice, Sydenham, London

Hardie, M.A., F.H.A., Mr. M. C., Director the Hospital Centre

Haywood, Mr Harold, Director of Education and Training, National Association of Youth Clubs

Health Visitors Association

Hertfordshire Council of Social Service

Hertfordshire Probation and Aftercare Department

Hobman, Mr David, Director, Social Work Advisory Service

Home Office

Hoodless, Mrs E., Deputy Director, Community Service Volunteers

Hunter, Miss E., Tutor and Adviser in Social Studies, University of London

Inner London Education Authority London School Care Service: Playgroups Association

* Institute of Medical Social Workers
* Institute of Social Welfare
* International Voluntary Service

Invalid Children's Aid Association

Jackson, Mrs B., Organizer, Manchester Youth and Community Service

* Jewish Welfare Board

Joint University Council for Social and Public Administration

Jones, O.B.E., Mr David, Senior Lecturer, Community Social Work, National Institute for Social Work Training

Kelham, House of the Sacred Mission

King, Mrs Chrystal, Organizer of Volunteers, Fulbourn Hospital, Cambridge
* Kingstanding Settlement, Birmingham
* Lady Margaret Hall Settlement
* Langley House Trust, Winchester
Le Gros Clark, Mr F.
* Lions International
Liverpool Personal Service Society
London Borough of Hounslow
London Council of Social Service
Manchester Council of Social Service
Manchester and Salford CSS, Youth and Community Services
* Mayflower Service Enterprise, Leicester
* Methodist Association of Youth Clubs
Miles, Miss J., Chairman, Playgroups Committee of Save the Children Fund
Ministry of Health
Ministry of Social Security
Moral Welfare Workers Association
* Mortlake and East Sheen Fellowship Service
* National Association for the Care and Resettlement of Offenders
* National Association for Mental Health
* National Association of Probation Officers
* National Association of Youth Clubs
* National Childbirth Trust
* National Citizens Advice Bureaux Council
* National Committee for Commonwealth Immigrants
* National Council of Associated Children's Homes
National Council of Social Service
* National Council of Voluntary Child Care Organizations
* National Federation of Women's Institutes
National Institute for Social Work Training
National League of the Blind
National Marriage Guidance Council
* National Old People's Welfare Council
* National Playing Fields Association
* National Society for Mentally Handicapped Children

* Neighbours Unlimited, Abingdon
  Newton, Mr George, Senior Lecturer, Social Work Training, National Institute for Social Work Training
* Northampton Wives and Families Group
  Pre-School Playgroups Association
* Prisoners' Wives Service
  Riches, Mr Graham, [formerly] Secretary of Association of London Housing Estate Groups
* Richmond Fellowship
* Ripon and Bradford Diocesan Police Court Mission
  Rocha, Mrs Jan, Social Investigation for the King's Fund
* Rotary International of Great Britain and Ireland
* Royal National Institute for the Blind
* Royal National Institute for the Deaf
* St Leonards Housing Association
  St Margaret's House Bethnal Green
* St Martin in the Fields Social Service Unit
* Samaritans Inc.
  Sanctuary, Mr G., National Secretary, National Marriage Guidance Council
* Save the Children Fund
  Sheffield Council of Churches
  Sheffield Diocesan Council for Social Responsibility
  Sheffield Probation and Aftercare Department
  Simon Community, Headquarters and Exeter Branch
  Smith, M.B.E., Mrs Muriel, Head of Community Development Department, London Council of Social Service
* Society of Medical Officers of Health
* Society of Mental Welfare Officers
* Soldiers, Sailors and Airmen's Families Association
* Standing Conference of Councils of Social Service
* Standing Conference of National Voluntary Youth Organizations
  Standing Conference of Organizations of Social Workers
* Standing Conference of Societies Registered for Adoption
  Steen, Mr Anthony, Director, Young Volunteer Force Foundation
  Stevenson, Miss Olive, Reader in Applied Social Studies in the University of Oxford

* Stortford Christian Service

Stroh, Mrs Katrin

Swift, Dr G. F., Department of Adult Education, University of Liverpool

* Talbot Settlement
* Task Force
* Teamwork Associates
* Time and Talents Association

Toxteth Community Council

* Toynbee Hall

Unilever Pensioners Association

* Union of Girls Schools for Social Service

United Community Funds and Councils of America

* University of Bristol Settlement
* Voluntary Help Scheme, Leicester

Ward, Miss M., Senior Lecturer in Social Work, City of Birmingham College of Commerce

Welfare Department of East Riding of Yorkshire

Willcocks, Dr A. J., Senior Lecturer in Social Science, University of Nottingham

Winnicott, Mrs C., Director of Child Care Training, Home Office

* Women's Royal Voluntary Service

Wright, Mr R. C., Chief Professional Adviser, Council for Training in Social Work

Yorkshire Working Party on the Training of Voluntary Workers

* Young Men's Christian Association

Young Volunteer Force Foundation

* Young Women's Christian Association

APPENDIX II

Notes on the Questionnaire sent to Voluntary Organizations using Voluntary Workers

(Copies of the questionnaire can be obtained from: The National Institute For Social Work Training, Mary Ward House, 5–7, Tavistock Place, London, W.C.1)

1. The organizations to which this questionnaire was sent varied widely in size, structure and purpose, and in the number of separate units or local branches which each represented. It was left to each organization to decide whether to deal with the questionnaire at local or at national level; and to select a sample of units or branches to which the questionnaire should be sent if the size of the organization made it impracticable to obtain and collate replies from all.

2. In our analysis of the questionnaires a sample was taken of replies received from organizations which had sent in a large number of local replies; but we must emphasize that it was not our intention to provide statistical material and that the material which emerges, while useful and illuminating, and suggestive of matters requiring further discussion, must not be taken to be more than this.

3. Fifty-one organizations were approached and asked to complete the questionnaire, and 38 of these did so. Of those who did not do so, a number explained that their use of volunteers was marginal or irrelevant to the enquiry, while four felt unable to complete the questionnaire as it stood but gave some information which could be used in other ways. Five arrived too late for analysis.

4. The replies which were returned can be classified as follows:
   I. Replies from local units of national organizations: 205 received.
   II. Comprehensive national or regional replies from national organizations: 15 received.

III. Replies from autonomous local bodies forming part of a national federation: (for example members of the British Association of Residential Settlements): 42 received.

5. A sample of 58 replies out of the 205 in group I were analysed, together with all of those in groups II and III, 115 in all.

Special Studies and Other Sources of Information about Volunteers and their Work

1. *Camden Council of Social Service, 1966 (Feb.)*
   An investigation into the selection, placing and training of voluntary workers in Hampstead.

   Information obtained from 24 statutory and voluntary organizations, and from 74 individual volunteers.

2. *City of Birmingham College of Commerce, 1967 (Summer term)*
   An enquiry by first-year students on the Certificate in Social Work Course into the voluntary social service undertaken by people living in three blocks of flats in Birmingham.

3. *The Institute of Community Studies, 1967 (November)*
   Voluntary workers in 6 organizations.

   A study of 114 volunteers working for local branches of 6 national voluntary organizations: 3 of these branches were in London, 1 on the outskirts of London, 1 in a new town in the Home Counties, and 1 in a provincial county town. There were 20 volunteers from each of 5 organizations and 14 from the sixth.

4. *King Edward's Hospital Fund for London, 1968*
   Organizers of Voluntary Services in Hospitals.

   A study of the work of full-time organizers of voluntary service in 10 general and 3 psychiatric hospitals; including information obtained from replies by 86 volunteers to a questionnaire on themselves and their work.

5. *Liverpool University: Department of Adult Education, 1967 (Nov.)*
   Voluntary Workers in Liverpool.

A study of paid and voluntary workers in 60 voluntary organizations in the City of Liverpool, affiliated to the Liverpool Council of Social Service: 429 workers were included, of whom 176 were paid and 253 were voluntary workers.

6. *Manchester and Salford Council of Social Service, and Manchester Youth and Community Service, 1967 (Sept.)*
A survey of the preparation and training of voluntary workers in the City of Manchester.

Information obtained from 77 statutory and voluntary bodies in Manchester, using approximately 7610 voluntary workers.

7. *University of Nottingham: Department of Applied Social Science, 1967*

Voluntary worker survey.

A preliminary report of a survey carried out in two areas near Nottingham.

A random sample of the population was interviewed, 282 from one area and 293 from the other, of whom 89 claimed to be doing active voluntary work.

8. *Portsmouth College of Technology: Department of Liberal Studies, 1965 (May)*
Attitudes towards voluntary social work in the City of Portsmouth.

A report based on interviews with 622 people, selected at random from the population aged 15 and over: 188 of these claimed to be doing voluntary work, but this included work which was 'spontaneous, as between neighbours and friends, or private, within the confines of family relationships'. The number who described themselves as doing 'public' work, i.e. work carried out in connection with some organization, was 66.

———

The volunteers who were interviewed in the study carried out by the Institute of Community Studies; in groups, by members of the Committee; or individually on behalf of the Committee, represented the following organizations and services:

British Red Cross Society
Citizens' Advice Bureaux
Community Service Volunteers
Disabled, Workers for the
Family Planning Association
Hospital Volunteers
International Voluntary Service
Marriage Guidance Council
Old People's Welfare
Probation and After-Care
Psychiatric Clubs
Samaritans
School Care Organization (Inner London)
Simon Community
Spastics Society
St John's Ambulance Brigade
Women's Royal Voluntary Service

o

209

Examples of Training Courses
(abbreviated from original notices)

a (i) *General background courses about social needs and services*

Mid-Herts. College of Further Education
SOCIAL SERVICE AND THE SOCIAL WORKER

An introductory course of twelve evening lectures, arranged in conjunction with the Welwyn Garden City Council of Social Service, for voluntary social workers and those interested in becoming engaged in voluntary social work.

The course commences on: Wednesday January 8, 1969, at 7.00 p.m. and is held weekly. Course fee: £2. (It may be possible to obtain a refund of part of the course fee for persons from organizations affiliated to the Council of Social Service.)

Session	Subject
1	(a) Introduction to the course
	(b) Background to 'The Welfare State'
2	The Role of the Voluntary Organization and Voluntary Worker
3	Services for the Family and Children
4	The Youth Service
5	The Family and Community Care
6	Social Work with Groups
7	Social Work with Individuals
8	Services for the Offender
9	Health and Welfare Services provided by Herts. C.C.
10	The Sick and their Special Need
11	Opportunities for Service
12	Evaluation of Course

Note: Each session will be of two hours duration, and will be introduced by a specialist in the particular subject. Students will be given every opportunity to question speakers, and discuss with them questions raised.

In order to ensure continuity a Course Tutor will be present at every session. The Course Tutor will also organize visits if there is sufficient demand.

(ii) *Introduction to Voluntary Social Work*

Adult Education Centre, Leicester, 1968
Tutor: Mr M. Laxton. Organizer, Leicester Family Service Unit.

Syllabus

Lecture 1 Introduction—purpose and scope of the course

Lecture 2, 3, 4, 5 Factors influencing normal human growth

Lecture 6, 7, 8, 9 Helping people with their problems—principles and approach

Lecture 10 Some ethical aspects of social work

Lecture 11 Case discussion (case material to be provided)

Lecture 12 Discussion—summing up the first session

The second term in the main is concerned with current social problems and the services that are provided to meet these difficulties. Lecturers are drawn from the services concerned.

Lecture 13 Relationship between the voluntary and statutory services—the role of the Council of Social Service.

Lecture 14 The work of the WRVS, Red Cross and Citizens Advice Bureau

Lecture 15 The child in need—the role of the Child Care Officer

Lecture 16 The emotionally disturbed child—the role of the Psychiatric Social Worker

Lecture 17 The adolescent—the role of the Youth Worker

Lecture 18 The young offender—the role of the Probation Officer

Lecture 19 The mentally ill—the role of the Mental Welfare Officer

Lecture 20 The problem of the problem family—the role of the family social worker

Lecture 21 The aged and physically handicapped—the role of the geriatric and welfare services

Lecture 22 Social benefits—an outline of the development of social security and basic entitlements to families

Lecture 23 The community work approach to social problems

Lecture 24 Prospects for the voluntary social worker—concluding survey and summing up

b. *Course specifically intended for workers in the social services, but of a fairly general type*

Birmingham Council of Social Service
SOCIAL WORK AND THE VOLUNTARY WORKER

This course has been specially designed to assist voluntary workers who are, or will shortly be, engaged in interviewing, home visiting and general welfare work for the Council of Social Service and similar organizations.

It has been arranged in conjunction with the Birmingham Branch of the Workers' Education Association and will be held on *Wednesday evenings*, at 161 Corporation Street at 7.30 p.m. beginning on October 9, 1968.

The Course will consist of ten talks followed by discussion and will cover a wide range of the kind of problems to be met with by voluntary workers in their efforts to help people. Wherever possible the course will be based on discussion of actual cases and problem situations met with in everyday work and those attending will be encouraged to present their own cases. Guidance will be given on techniques of interviewing, fact finding, writing up of reports and the use of the various social services.

Tutor: Mr R. Burgess, Divisional Social Welfare Officer, Birmingham Welfare Department (formerly Secretary and Senior Caseworker to the Personal Service Committee).

The course will aim to cover the following range of topics.

The Special Role of the Voluntary Worker
The relationship between voluntary and professional workers. Special problems of the volunteer. Different ways of 'helping'.

People and their Problems
Needing and 'wanting' help and ways in which problems are presented. The process of application or referral.

Doing the Job
Receiving clients. Interviewing. Home visiting. Writing reports. Using the Case Committee.

Problems of Money and Material need
What is poverty today? Assessing income and expenditure. Social Security benefits. Rent arrears and eviction. Gas, electricity and commercial debts. Court Orders. The emotional significance of money.

Problems of Personal Adequacy and Family Breakdown
Divorce, desertion, and separation. Unemployment. Physical and mental illness. The Community Care services.

Using the Social Services
Special aspects of the services in Birmingham. When, where and whom to contact.

The Future Pattern of the Social Services
Significance of the recent report of the 'Seebohm Committee' and its effects on voluntary services.

Reading List: Guidance will be given throughout the Course on special books and pamphlets useful to Voluntary Workers.

Fees: The fee for this course will be 10s., payable in advance. Voluntary workers with the Council of Social Service are exempt from payment.

c. *Training provided by individual organizations for their own workers who will be undertaking specialized work*

(i) *Youth Resettlement Project*
Community action for homeless young offenders

The Youth Resettlement Project has been initiated by the Inner London Probation and After-care Service and Teamwork Associates as an attempt to involve the community in the after-care of homeless young people released from borstals, detention centres and prisons. Such people are subject to supervision by probation officers for periods of between one and two years after release. Volunteers are urgently needed to help in any of the following ways: (1) By offering to write to or visit a homeless boy or girl during their custodial sentence and by keeping in touch with them afterwards. (2) By stimulating interest and support in their youth club, church group or other voluntary organization. (3) By offering temporary or more permanent accommodation, or by encouraging friends to do so.

How to begin: Without preparation and support, most people would hesitate to take on such tasks. If you are interested in any aspect of the Project and feel you may have something to offer, please contact one of the Project Officers who will be glad to discuss it with you. If you are 20 or over and would like to offer individual help (as in (i) (1) above), you are invited to enrol for the next preparation course which is due to begin on April 15th (details below). On completion, you may have the opportunity of applying to be accredited as a 'voluntary associate' by a selection panel, although no obligation is entailed. Vacancies on the course are limited and early application is advisable. Suitable married couples will be especially welcome.

Support: Voluntary associates will subsequently be able to learn from their experience through discussions with probation officers and in small groups. They will also be welcome at conferences and further courses as members of Teamwork Associates.

PREPARATION COURSES FOR VOLUNTARY ASSOCIATES
April 15–June 3, 1969
Co-Tutors: Mr P. N. Kidner, Miss P. Diamond, Mr N. Rose

PROGRAMME	LECTURERS
1. *April 15th* (a) Lecture—'The offender and the community'. (b) Small groups—general discussion.	E. G. Pratt, Assistant Principal Probation Officer
2. *April 22nd* (a) Lecture—'Why volunteer?' (b) Small groups—case discussion.	N. Ingram-Smith, St. Martin-in-the-Fields Social Service Unit
3. *April 29th* (a) Lecture—'Aims and methods of Borstal training'. (b) General discussion.	D. Leach, Deputy Governor, H.M. Borstal, Dover.

VISITS OF OBSERVATION TO H.M. BORSTALS

4. *May 6th* (a) Small groups—discussion on visits (b) Lecture—After-care—'the Second Sentence'.	J. Pannell, Senior Probation Officer
5. *May 13th* (a) Discussion panel—'Building a relationship'. (b) Small groups—case discussion.	Liaison Probation Officers (After-care Registry and Resettlement Unit)
6. *May 20th* (a) Lecture—'Role of the voluntary associate'. (b) Small groups—Discussion with experienced associates.	P. N. Kidner, Project Officer.
7. *May 27th* (a) Discussion panel—'Problems of the unattached'.	Miss M. Osmond (formerly of Kensal Project) D. Hughes (formerly of Blenheim Project)
8. *June 3rd* (a) Small groups—'Guidelines for voluntary associates'. (b) Course review	by the Co-Tutors

All meetings will be held at the After-Care Registry and Resettlement Unit, 289 Borough High Street, S.E.1. from 6.30 p.m.–8.30 p.m. (Tuesday evenings)

(ii) *Information Course: 'Services for the Elderly'—Mitcham Old People's Welfare Committee*
Evening Course: 7.30 p.m. at Mitcham Grammar School for Boys.
Afternoon Course: 2.00 p.m. at 326, London Road, Mitcham.

Chaired by Mrs Billinge, Visiting Organizer, Mitcham O.P.W.C.

1.	Oct. 3rd, 7.30 Oct. 4th, 2 p.m.	Purpose of the Course Introductions from the floor. Film: 'No Milk To-day', showing voluntary services provided by one O.P.W.C. (Sevenoaks). Discussion.	H. E. Lobstein, Field Officer for Training, National Old People's Welfare Council.
2.	Oct. 10th, 7.30 Oct. 11th, 2 p.m.	The function of statutory and voluntary social workers, and how they can help each other.	W. Hutchinson, Chief Welfare Officer, L. B. of Merton.
3.	Oct. 17th, 7.30 Oct. 18th, 2 p.m.	Panel Discussion: (a) Social Security allowances: why some old people do not receive them, and how voluntary workers can help.	L. Foster, Manager, Ministry of Social Security.
		(b) The Meals on Wheels Service, and how it can be used to discover and report impending deterioration before it is too late.	Mrs L. Forsdick, W.R.V.S.
		(c) The Home Help Service; how a neighbour can cook a meal for an old person or provide other services, and how this may be financed.	Miss M. Faraday, Home Help Organiser.
4.	Oct. 24th, 7.30 Oct. 25th, 2 p.m.	Some aspects of the emotional needs of old people.	Mrs Silcock, Psychiatric Social Worker, Netherne Hospital.
5.	Oct. 31st, 7.30 Nov. 1st, 2 p.m.	The work of the geriatric department. What happens when an old person is discharged from hospital, and what help can be provided by voluntary workers.	Mrs Pillinger, Geriatric Social Worker, St. Helier Hospital.
6.	Nov. 7th, 7.30 Nov. 8th, 2 p.m.	Practical problems of old people living alone (e.g. health, diet, accident prevention, etc.)	(Nov. 7) Dr M. Susman, Public Health Dept. (Nov. 8) Miss Richards, Superintendent Health Visitor, L.B. of Merton.
7.	Nov. 14th, 7.30 Nov. 15th, 2 p.m.	Discussion in small groups (use 'talking points' lists). Reporting back from groups. Linking the Course to practical work in the community. Reports to sponsoring organizations, and arrangement of possible follow-up meetings to discuss plans resulting from these reports.	Mrs Billinge, Visiting Organizer, Mitcham O.P.W.C.

Suggestions For Further Reading

BATTEN, T. R., *The Non-directive Approach in Group and Community Work*. O.U.P., 1967.

BEVERIDGE, LORD, *Voluntary Action*. London: Allen & Unwin, 1948.

BIRMINGHAM COUNCIL OF CHRISTIAN CHURCHES, *Responsibility in the Welfare State*. Birmingham: Council of Christian Churches, 1961.

THE BOARD FOR SOCIAL RESPONSIBILITY OF THE NATIONAL ASSEMBLY OF THE CHURCH OF ENGLAND, *The Church and the Social Services*. London: Church Information Office, 1969.

BUGLER, Jeremy, 'The Volunteer Upsurge', in *New Society*. London: New Science Publications, 1965.

CALOUSTE GULBENKIAN FOUNDATION, *Community Work and Social Change. A report on training*. London: Longmans, Green & Co. Ltd, 1968.

CENTRAL CHURCHES GROUP, *The Caring Community*. London: The National Council of Social Service, 1966.

CLARK, Dr D. H., 'Fulbourn Hospital, Cambridge'. An article on voluntary workers in a psychiatric hospital, in *The Lancet*. London: Lancet, 1966.

CLARK, F. Le Gros, *Work, Age and Leisure*. London: Michael Joseph, 1966.

DICKSON, Mora and Alec, *Count us in*. London: Dobson, 1967.

DONNISON, D. V., *Social Policy and Administration*. London: Allen & Unwin, 1965.

ERIKSON, Erik, H., *Youth, Change and Challenge*. New York: Basic Books, 1963.

GILLETTE, Arthur, *1,000,000 Volunteers: The Story of Volunteer*

Youth Service. Harmondsworth: Penguin Books, 1968.

GOETSCHIUS, George W., *Working with Community Groups*. London: Routledge & Kegan Paul, 1969.

GOETSCHIUS and TASH, *Working with Unattached Youth*. London: Routledge & Kegan Paul, 1967.

GREEN, Laurence, *Parents and Teachers. Partners or Rivals?* London: Allen & Unwin, 1968.

HANCOCK, A. and WILLMOTT, P. (Ed.), *The Social Workers*. London: B.B.C., 1965.

HETHERINGTON, Sir Hector, *The Role of the Voluntary Services in Contemporary Britain*. London: The National Council of Social Service, 1963.

HEYWOOD, Dr Jean, *The Social Services and Society*. Address given at Annual Conference of the Association of Children's Officers, 1968.

JEFFERYS, Margot, *An Anatomy of Social Welfare Services*. London: Michael Joseph, 1965.

KEELEY, B., *1020 Playgroups*. London: Pre-school Playgroup Association, 1968.

KEITH-LUCAS, Alan, *The Church and Social Welfare*. Philadelphia: The Westminster Press, 1962.

KUENSTLER, P., *Community Organisation in Great Britain*. London: Faber, 1961.

LEVIN, Herman, 'Volunteers in Social Welfare: the Challenge of their Future', in *Social Work*. New York: National Association of Social Workers, 1969.

LONDON COUNCIL OF SOCIAL SERVICE, *Some Opportunities for Voluntary Social Service in London*. London: London Council of Social Service, 1967.

MARRIS, P. and REIN, M., *Dilemmas of Social Reform*. London: Routledge & Kegan Paul, 1967.

MARSHALL, T. H., *Sociology at the Cross Roads*. London: Heinemann, 1963.

MORRIS, Mary, *Voluntary Organisations and Social Progress*. London: Gollancz, 1955.

MORRIS, Mary, *A Study of Halifax*. London: The National Council of Social Service, 1965.

MORRIS, Mary, *Social Enterprise*. London: The National Council of Social Service, 1962.

217

NAYLOR, Harriet H., *Volunteers Today. Finding, training and working with them.* New York: N.Y. Association Press, 1967.

OWEN, David, *English Philanthropy 1660–1960.* O.U.P., 1965.

RICHES, Graham, 'We are our own Social Workers', in *Social Service Quarterly.* London: N.C.S.S. 1967.

ROOFF, M., *Voluntary Societies and Social Policy.* London: Routledge & Kegan Paul, 1957.

ROSENBLATT, A., 'Interest of Older Persons in Volunteer Activities', in *Social Work.* New York: National Association of Social Workers, 1966.

SANCTUARY, G., *Marriage Under Stress.* London: Allen & Unwin, 1968.

SILLS, D. M., *The Volunteers.* New York: Free Press, 1957.

SLACK, Kathleen M., *Social Administration and the Citizen.* London: Michael Joseph, 1966.

SPENCER, John, *Stress and Release in an Urban Estate.* London: Tavistock Publications, 1964.

TIMMS, Noel, *Rootless in the City.* London: Bedford Square Press, 1969.

TITMUSS, Richard M., *Commitment to Welfare.* London: Allen & Unwin, 1968.

UNITED NATIONS, *European Seminar on Functions and Training of Voluntary Social Welfare Workers.* Report. Geneva: United Nations, 1967.

UNITED NATIONS, *Report of a United Nations Study Group on The Functions and Preparation of Voluntary Workers in the Social Services. Cambridge, 1967.* London: National Council of Social Service, 1967.

VARAH, Chad, *The Samaritans.* London: Constable, 1965.

WALLIS, J. H., *Someone to turn to: a description of the remedial work of The National Marriage Guidance Council.* London: Routledge & Kegan Paul, 1961.

WOODROOFE, Kathleen, *From Charity to Social Work.* London: Routledge & Kegan Paul, 1962.

YOUNG, M. and MCGEENEY, P., *Learning Begins at Home.* London: Routledge & Kegan Paul, 1968.

APPENDICES

Government Publications (H.M.S.O.)

Community Service and the Curriculum. The Schools Council, Working paper No. 17.

Service by Youth. Report of a Committee of the Youth Service Development Council. (Bessey Report), 1966.

A Guide to Voluntary Service by David Hobman, Revised 1969.

Department of Education and Science: *Children and their Primary Schools.* 2 vols. (Plowden [Lady] Report), 1966.

The Place of Voluntary Service in After Care. Second Report of Working Party. (Reading Report), 1967.

Residential provision for homeless discharged offenders. Report of Working Party. (Reading Report), 1966.

Report of the Committee on Local Authority & Allied Personal Social Services CMD 3703. (Seebohm Report), 1968.

Report of the Working Party on Social Workers in the Local Authority Health and Welfare Services. (Younghusband Report), 1959.

INDEX

Note: References are to page, not paragraph, numbers. The Appendices are lightly indexed.

Compiled by Miss Alison Hodgson